HERE WE ARE . . . ON ROUTE 66

HERE WE ARE . . . ON

ROUTE 66

A JOURNEY DOWN AMERICA'S MAIN STREET

Jim Hinckley

motorbooks

Brimming with creative inspiration, how-to projects, and useful information to enrich your everyday life, Quarto Knows is a favorite destination for those pursuing their interests and passions. Visit our site and dig deeper with our books into your area of interest: Quarto Creates, Quarto Cooks, Quarto Homes, Quarto Lives, Quarto Drives, Quarto Explores, Quarto Gifts, or Quarto Kids.

Inspiring | Educating | Creating | Entertaining

First Published in 2022 by Motorbooks, an imprint of The Quarto Group, 100 Cummings Center, Suite 265-D, Beverly, MA 01915, USA.
T (978) 282-9590 F (978) 283-2742 QuartoKnows.com

Motorbooks titles are also available at discount for retail, wholesale, promotional, and bulk purchase. For details, contact the Special Sales Manager by email at specialsales@quarto.com or by mail at The Quarto Group, Attn: Special Sales Manager, 100 Cummings Center, Suite 265-D, Beverly, MA 01915, USA.

26 25 24 23 22 22   1 2 3 4 5

ISBN: 978-0-7603-7199-2

Digital edition published in 2022
eISBN: 978-0-7603-7200-5

Library of Congress Control Number: 2021946071

Acquiring Editor: Dennis Pernu
Series Creative Director: Laura Drew
Cover Design and Page Layout: Cindy Samargia Laun
Cover Art: adapted from Shutterstock

Printed in China

CONTENTS

PREFACE AND ACKNOWLEDGMENTS

Route 66 is no mere highway. Route 66 associations in more than ten countries organize events, host Route 66 tours, and publish travel guides. At the 2018 European Route 66 Festival in Zlin, Czech Republic, an estimated 20,000 people were in attendance from ten countries including Brazil. The innovative Route 66 Navigation app and Mother Road Route 66 Passport that has transformed the traveler's experience on this storied highway was developed by a gentleman in Bratislava, Slovakia.

Tulsa, Oklahoma, has initiated an ambitious program to restore a colorful neon glow to the Route 66 corridor in that city. All along the highway from Chicago to Santa Monica, once derelict motels have been given a new lease on life. Towns are using the international fascination with Route 66 as a catalyst for historic district revitalization and economic development.

Even though the highway is lined with tangible links to centuries of history, Route 66 is often viewed as America's longest attraction rather than as a string of time capsules. The focus is often myopic and centers on neon, tailfins, and a romanticized view of American life in the 1950s.

With this book, I would like to introduce you to a few special communities and to Route 66 as the world's longest museum. I also want to present this storied road as a *living* time capsule and add depth as well as context to the story of the most famous highway in America.

Finally, my name may be on the cover and title page. And I did write every word. But it was my dearest friend of nearly forty years who made this work possible. Without her support, insight, patience, and encouragement, transforming an idea into a book would not be possible.

And of course, credit must also be given to the editors. They are the people who catch my mistakes, ensure that I do not become too long-winded, and ferret out transpositions or errors.

I would also be remiss if a shout-out were not given to the international legion of Route 66 enthusiasts. Their infectious enthusiasm and passion have fueled my ideas that became manifest in this book. And they have provided valuable assistance as well as illustrations.

INTRODUCTION:
THE MAIN STREET OF AMERICA

Judge J. M. Lowe, president of the National Old Trails Road Association, often referred to the National Old Trails Road as the Main Street of America. It was an apt descriptor, for this early highway that stretched from Maryland to California was knit from the nation's historic roads and trails including the National Road, Santa Fe Trail, Beale Wagon Road, and Old Spanish Trail.

In early 1927, Cyrus Avery and a group of business leaders with vision established the U.S. Highway 66 Association. The organization had several goals including lobbying to have the highway paved for its entire length between Chicago and Los Angeles. Equally as important was creation of initiatives to develop tourism along the highway corridor.

One of the organization's first projects was a marketing campaign that billed US 66 as "The Main Street of America." As the highway was the literal main street in many of the communities along the highway corridor, this moniker was as fitting to Route 66 as it had been for the National Old Trails Road.

Today, in the era of a Route 66 renaissance, it remains an apt descriptor. America's most famous highway is firmly rooted in the past. But it is also linked to the future as is evidenced by the establishment of the world's only electric vehicle museum in Kingman, Arizona, and the installation of charging stations at historic sites along the highway corridor.

With these profiles of select Route 66 communities, I illustrate why Route 66 was, and is, the Main Street of America. I present the most famous highway in America as the crossroads of the past and future. So, here we are . . . on Route 66.

CHAPTER ONE

ILLINOIS

LAND OF LINCOLN

ROMEOVILLE

Route 66 followed Joliet Road through Romeoville from 1926 to 1939. When the highway was realigned along the current path of I-55, the original corridor was signed as "Alt 66" through 1966.

But when Route 66 was certified along Joliet Road, it was merely the latest manifestation of a trade corridor that was centuries old. The Native American trail system that connected the Mississippi River and Lake Michigan and was augmented by a network of rivers grew in importance with European exploration and colonization of the area.

Historians believe that the first non–Native American men to travel the forested trail along the Des Plaines River through the modern Romeoville area was Jesuit missionary Father Jacques Marquette. He was accompanied on the expedition of 1673 by the cartographer Louis Jolliet.

The 101-acre (40.9 ha) Isle a la Cache was acquired from the Forest Preserve District of Will County between 1982 and 2014. The preserve is a component of the Des Plaines River preservation system that conserves 2,400 acres

(971.2 ha) of forested woodland. Archeologists believe that the area was used by French explorers in the 1700s to cache the supplies and the goods that they traded with Native Americans.

The Isle a la Cache Museum is an interactive complex that blends cultural heritage and natural history. It allows visitors to experience the eighteenth century when this was a focal point of the "Illinois Country" fur trade between French explorers and the Potawatomi.

Jolliet noted in his travel journal that a canal connecting Lake Michigan with the Illinois River would create an almost unhindered waterway to the Mississippi River. In 1816, that idea became manifest when the United States Congress authorized funds for the survey and construction of the Illinois and Michigan Shipping Canal.

However, arrangements first had to be made with Native Americans for acquisition of a 20-mile (32.2 km)-wide strip of land. The agreement proved to be short lived as President Jackson's Indian Removal Act became law in 1830. This negated previous agreements and allowed for the relocation of Native American villages. In their place, new towns were laid out along the course of the proposed canal.

The canal's board of commissioners were empowered to set the route of the canal and to designate townships. Interestingly, Romeoville was first named Romeo. The village to the south was named Juliet but in 1845 was renamed Joliet.

Speculators purchased land in Romeo for $1.25 per acre (0.4 ha) in 1835. With announcement that construction of the canal would commence in Bridgeport in July 1836, that same land sold for $200 per acre (0.4 ha).

The Illinois and Michigan Canal was completed in 1848 and expanded between 1892 and 1900 with construction of the Chicago Drainage Canal between the Chicago River and Des Plaines River. It concluded its transportation operations in 1933 and was designated in 1984 as The Illinois and Michigan Canal National Heritage Area, which is considered an "outdoor museum," offering hiking, canoeing, and biking as well as interactive exhibits.

Agricultural products, dairy farming, and quarrying were the economic drivers in Romeoville

during its formative years. During its peak in the early twentieth century, two trainloads of limestone were being shipped from Romeoville every morning on the Chicago, Rock Island & Pacific Railroad. The limestone quarried at Romeoville was used in major construction projects throughout the state. The Illinois State Capitol Building in Springfield is one of the most famous buildings constructed with this stone.

In the mid-1850s, the railroad magnified Romeoville's access to markets in St. Louis and Chicago. Then, on May 18, 1905, Illinois became one of the first states to establish a commission to address its rural road system. In the decades that followed, this would have a major impact on Romeoville as it led to completion of a paved road connecting Chicago to St. Louis in 1921. This would become the course for Route 66 in 1926.

A tangible link to the city's agricultural heritage and its connection to Route 66 is White Fence Farm, a restaurant and museum complex. The restaurant dates to the early 1920s and was established by Stuyvesant "Jack" Peabody. Stuyvesant was the son of Peabody Coal Company founder Francis S. Peabody and CEO of the company at the time.

The restaurant was opened on acreage opposite his Lemont horse farm on Joliet Road. It soon became a popular stop for travelers on the newly paved state highway connecting Chicago with Joliet and St. Louis. The restaurant's specialty was creamy milk products produced at local dairies, including ice cream, and hamburgers.

The restaurant received favorable reviews and recommendations from Duncan Hines as well as AAA. With the repeal of Prohibition, Peabody expanded the dinner menu and established a cellar with a wide array of California wines. After Peabody's death in 1946, the restaurant was leased to several operators until the family sold the property in 1954.

The restaurant has been owned and operated by the Hastert family since that time. Fried chicken has become their specialty.

The restaurant has been expanded over the years. It now has seating for more than 1,000 customers. Side galleries house an antique car collection and a display of rare original Currier & Ives prints, among other nostalgic displays. During the summer, the restaurant has an outdoor petting zoo, a tradition established in the 1960s.

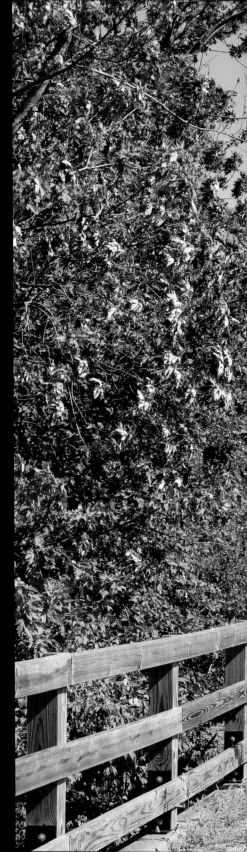

"ROADS WERE MADE FOR JOURNEYS, NOT DESTINATIONS."

—CONFUCIUS

PONTIAC

In Pontiac, Route 66 followed a twisted course through town on Pontiac Road and Division, Lincoln, and Ladd Streets. In the 1940s, a bypass was built to funnel an ever-increasing flow of traffic away from the congested city center.

Towering over the historic heart of the city is the courthouse, an architectural masterpiece built in 1874. A clock tower was added in 1892. The Civil War Monument honoring "the Soldiers and Sailors of Livingston County" on the courthouse square was dedicated by President Theodore Roosevelt in 1903.

At the opposite side of the square is a statue of Abraham Lincoln that was designed by sculptor Rick Harney. It was dedicated on June 23, 2006. The life-size bronze work commemorates Lincoln's first visit to Pontiac in 1840 as a 31-year-old lawyer.

These are but a few of the many treasures that are tangible links to the city's rich and colorful history. Built in 1857, the Jones House is the oldest remaining brick home in the city. This uniquely styled house was placed on the National Register of Historic Places on May 5, 1978. Now a museum, the Yost House built in

1898 retains many original furnishings as it was owned by the same family for more than one hundred years.

The Jason W. Strevell House built in 1854 is a tangible link to the city's prominence in the mid-nineteenth century. Strevell served as a Republican in the Illinois House of Representatives. He also served as a United States Senator and was a member of the electoral college that elected President Hayes.

Strevell was an associate and friend of Abraham Lincoln. On the evening of January 27, 1860, Lincoln spoke at the Pontiac Young Men's Literary Society and spent the evening at the Strevell house. After dinner, the conversation turned to politics, and Strevell suggested that Lincoln could be selected as the Republican Party's presidential candidate at the upcoming party convention.

Not all the sites in Pontiac are tangible links to such pivotal moments in history. As an example, there are three bridges for pedestrian traffic over the Vermilion River. The planking has been replaced but the oldest bridge was built in July 1898 by the Joliet Bridge Company.

It connects Riverside Drive to Play Park. The 190-foot (58 m)-long bridge is supported by cables swung from concrete and iron piers. It was built to allow workers living on the south side of Pontiac access to the shoe factories.

The second bridge is of particular interest. Built in 1926, it connects Play Park to Chautauqua Park. The bridge provided residents with easy access to the Camp-Humiston Memorial Swimming Pool that opened in 1925. It also provided additional access to the annual Chautauqua assemblies.

The third Swinging Bridge is a relatively recent addition. It was built in 1978 by Illinois Contractors, Inc., in Humiston-Riverside Park. This is the site of the nineteenth-century Bloomington, Pontiac & Joliet Electric Railway bridge.

The Chautauqua assemblies began in the summer of 1874 at Fair Point on Lake Chautauqua, New York. The Chautauqua brought entertainment and culture suitable for the entire family to rural communities. Performances included teachers, musicians, entertainers, preachers, and actors that performed in Shakespearean plays.

President Theodore Roosevelt praised the events and said, "The Chautauqua Movement is one of the most American things in America." During World War I, President Woodrow Wilson proclaimed the Chautauqua Assemblies an "integral part of the national defense."

The First Pontiac Chautauqua Assembly opened on July 29, 1898. The two-week event was so successful that it continued as one of the country's top Chautauqua assemblies for more than thirty years.

Visitors were able to listen to sermons from leading preachers and speeches from politicians. There were also lectures and demonstrations on world events, technology, science, and literature. Musicians, dancers that performed traditional dances from throughout the world, magicians, circus acts, and jugglers provided more lighthearted entertainment.

Explorers shared glass lantern slide shows that showcased exotic corners of the world such as Africa, China, the Middle East, and Australia. During some assemblies, full Broadway productions were presented.

Many scientific wonders were introduced to the rural population at the assemblies. As an example, many pioneering manufacturers provided demonstrations of new gasoline and steam powered tractors. The first motion picture shown in Pontiac took place at an assembly. Ironically, it was the motion picture, the radio, and more modern forms of entertainment that brought the Chautauqua events to an end in the 1920s.

The Route 66 renaissance has contributed greatly to the revitalization of the Pontiac historic district. And as evidenced by the brilliant murals, including one that recreates a Chautauqua Assembly promotion, it has also ignited a rediscovery of the city's colorful, rich, and diverse history.

A Route 66 landmark of note is the Old Log Cabin restaurant. Built in 1926, when the highway was realigned, the building was lifted from its foundation and turned to face the new highway.

Today, the village of Pontiac has come to symbolize how harnessing the resurgent interest in Route 66 can transform a community. A once faded business district littered with empty storefronts is now vibrant and colorful, with an array of eclectic shops, restaurants, and beautiful public art.

There are also diverse museums including the Pontiac-Oakland Automobile Museum, Livingston County War Museum, Route 66 Museum, and Museum of the Gilding Arts.

ATLANTA

Even during the pre-interstate era when Route 66 funneled a steady stream of travelers through town on SW and NE Arch Streets, Atlanta, Illinois, remained a small agricultural town. The town was established in 1853 under the name Xenia. However, the initial post office application was rejected as there was another town in Illinois by that name.

A *Guide Book to Highway 66* written by Jack Rittenhouse in 1946 noted that the town had a "garage, gas stations, cafes but no hotels or cabins." It was also noted that, "US 66 goes down one of the main business streets, past some very old store buildings, some dating to the 1850s."

The renewed interest in Route 66 sparked a revival in the town's diminutive business district, but it is the tangible links to Atlanta's past that make the village unique. The J. H. Hawes Elevator is an excellent example of the diverse historic sites of note. Added to the National Register of Historic Places on May 17, 1999, this is the only restored and operational wooden grain elevator in Illinois. It was built in 1903 along the Illinois & Midland Railroad to store locally farmed grain before shipping. Surprisingly, the elevator remained in operation until 1975.

Built in 1908, the Atlanta Public Library was designed by architect Paul A. Moratz. The octagonal

building built of dressed stone has only seven symmetrical sides. The front is dominated by a classic styled portico with Doric columns and a round arched entrance. The building is still used for its original purpose.

A clock tower built in 1978 stands on the library grounds. The Seth Thomas clock itself was originally installed in the Atlanta High School in 1909. It is hand wound every eight days. A window in the door that allowed visitors to watch the winding became a popular attraction for Route 66 travelers. This served as the catalyst for the revitalization of the historic business district.

On Arch Street on the Route 66 corridor, many of the buildings noted by Jack Rittenhouse in 1946 have been renovated. Dominating a block of historic storefronts is the Downey Building built by Alexander Downey in 1867. After losing his business in a fire that devasted the business district, Downey rebuilt with brick. Of Italianate design with characteristic arched windows on both of its two stories, the building became the namesake for Arch Street. It was built to house two stores behind a single façade.

Aside from Downey's store, the building initially housed the Exchange Bank of Atlanta. After the turn of the century, the father and son law firm of J. L. and Frank Bevan moved into the space. The building also served as the offices for the *Atlanta Argus*, the local paper, until it was extensively damaged by fire in 1973. After nearly a decade of abandonment, the heirs of the Bevan family donated their half of the building to the Atlanta Public Library and Museum.

Aside from Downey's store, the other side of the building has been used as a hardware store and grocery store. In 1934, Robert Adams renovated the building and opened the Palms Grill Cafe. On August 4th of that year, the *Atlanta Argus* announced "The Palms Grill, East Side Square—On US Route 66—Atlanta, Now Open for Business. Home Cooking, Quick Service, Courteous Treatment. Plate lunch 25 cents."

Listed in the National Register of Historic Places in 2004, the building underwent an extensive renovation. Until early 2020, it housed an operational recreation of the Palms Grill Cafe. The grill was included in the video series *Billy Connolly's Route 66* starring internationally acclaimed Scottish comedian Billy Connolly.

The building complex also houses two museums. One, Route 66

Arcade Museum, is an interactive collection of vintage pinball machines and historic electronic arcade machines. At the Atlanta Museum, the story of the town, including the Route 66 connection, is told through interesting exhibits. These include displays that highlight the town's association with Abraham Lincoln.

The Colaw Rooming House is a fascinating time capsule and an example of the city's innovative initiatives to capitalize on the interest in Route 66. Built around 1900, in the 1940s, it was transformed into a boarding house that rented rooms on a long-term basis to single teachers who worked in Atlanta. The home has been renovated to an appearance that mimics this era including the addition of a yellow-and-red themed 1940s-style kitchen. Rooms or the entire house is rented through Airbnb.

Adding to the town's Norman Rockwell feel is Route 66 Park. The former ticket office from the Atlanta Fair that was held between 1860 and 1929 is now used as an information booth in the park.

A lot created by the razing of a building is the site of another small park. It is dominated by a 19-foot (5.8 m)-tall Paul Bunyon statue (purposely spelled with an "o") clutching a giant hot dog. The statue was originally used to promote Bunyon's hot dog stand along Route 66 in Ogden, Illinois, for more than forty years. The statue was acquired by the city of Atlanta after the restaurant's closing in 2003.

> "WHEN YOU'RE TRAVELING, YOU ARE WHAT YOU ARE RIGHT THERE AND THEN. PEOPLE DON'T HAVE YOUR PAST TO HOLD AGAINST YOU. NO YESTERDAYS ON THE ROAD."
>
> —WILLIAM LEAST HEAT MOON

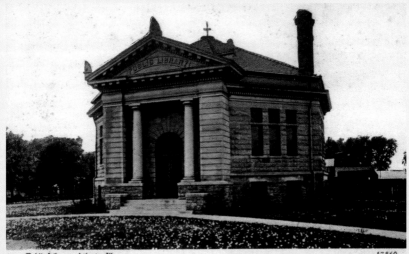

Public Library, Atlanta, Ill.   17860

SPRINGFIELD

Initially, Route 66 entered Springfield on Peoria Road and followed the course of Illinois Route 4 built in 1921. Route 66 also utilized 9th Street, Capital, 2nd Street, S Grand Avenue, Macarthur, Wabash, Chatham Road, and Woodside Road. The final alignment, now Business Loop 55, followed Peoria Road and traversed the city on 9th Street, 5th Street, 6th Street, Spruce Street, and Myrtle Street.

In 1821, a political compromise resulted in the site of Springfield being designated the temporary seat for Sangamon County. As a result, the community was initially named Sangamon Courthouse. Actual platting of the town site on Spring Creek commenced in 1823.

Amendment of the post office application approved on February 19, 1828, resulted in the name change to Springfield. In 1836, the town was designated the state capital.

The city will always be associated with Abraham Lincoln. The only home he ever owned still stands at Eighth and Jackson Streets and is maintained by the National Park Service. It is the centerpiece of a four-block historic district preserved to appear as it did when Abraham Lincoln lived here.

Lincoln's law office remains at 6th and Adams Streets. The depot from which he departed to Washington, D.C., as president elect, and returned after his assassination, is located at 10th and Monroe Streets. The Abraham Lincoln Presidential Library and Museum is located at 212 North 6th Street, an alignment of Route 66, and The Lincoln Tomb is at 1500 Monument Avenue.

The Old State Capitol located at 1 Old State Capitol Plaza is a reconstruction of the first statehouse located in Springfield. In this building, Abraham Lincoln practiced law, served as a legislator, and gave his famed *House Divided* speech on slavery on June 16, 1858.

The building was used as the center for state government until 1876. On February 10, 2007, Senator Barack Obama announced his candidacy for president of the United States on the Old State Capitol steps.

The Illinois Legislature authorized construction of the current state capitol building in 1867. The first state legislature session took place

in the building in 1877 even though it was not completed until 1888.

The city's association with Abraham Lincoln is in stark contrast to an incident known as the Springfield Race Riot. On the evening of August 14, 1908, simmering racial tensions exploded over a report that a Black man had been arrested for the assault of a white woman. This incident occurred shortly after a nonresident Black man named Joe James had been accused of murdering a white railroad engineer.

An angry mob gathered and stormed the jail, demanding that both men be turned over to them for lynching. When the mob learned that the police had secretly taken the prisoners out the back door and transported them to another town for safety, the riot commenced.

A restaurant owned by Harry Loper who had provided the automobile used by the sheriff was destroyed. The mob then moved into a Black business district and began smashing windows, destroying merchandise, and wrecking equipment. They then swept into a neighborhood called the Badlands and lynched Scott Burton, a Black barber.

The next evening, after learning that many African Americans had taken refuge at the state arsenal, the mob stormed the facility. They were driven off by troopers, but overtook another Black neighborhood where they lynched William Donegan, an 84-year-old businessman. Sporadic violence continued for several months. As news of this tragedy spread through the United States, it ultimately prompted the formation of the National Association for the Advancement of Colored People (NAACP), which fights for civil rights and equality for all people.

Possibly the most famous site associated with Route 66 in Springfield would be the Cozy Dog Drive In. Established by Edwin Waldmire Jr., father of renowned artist Robert "Bob" Waldmire, the Cozy Dog Drive In opened in 1949. It was relocated to its current location at 2935 S 6th Street, the site of the former Lincoln Motel, on Route 66 in 1996.

Lake Springfield is a 4,000-acre (1,618.7 ha) artificial lake constructed by the city of Springfield in the early 1930s. Lick Creek Wildlife Preserve located at the western end of Lake Springfield is a rare urban oasis of wooded hills and marsh land laced by hiking and off-road biking trails.

An interesting historic footnote associated with Lake Springfield is the ghost town of Cotton Hill. In an editorial published by *The Illinois State Journal* in November 1933, it was noted that, "Cotton Hill had its name from a pioneer effort to raise cotton in this county by Kentuckians who came to Sangamon county in 1835."

The small village was located on the Illinois Central Railroad, and after 1926, Route 66. In the late nineteenth century, the town had a pottery works. Before it was razed during construction of the lake, the town consisted of a blacksmith shop and a general store that also served as a post office.

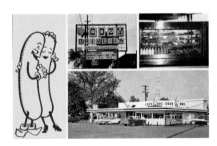

CARLINVILLE

In Carlinville, US 66 followed Illinois Route 4 through town. It coursed along 1st South Street one block from Main Street.

Thomas Carlin, governor of Illinois from 1838 to 1842, is the namesake for Carlinville. He was a veteran of the War of 1812 and had served as a captain of the Illinois militia during the Black Hawk War.

Almost the entire downtown business district surrounding the square and the residential district to the west has been listed on the National Register of Historic Places since 1976. A dominant feature of the downtown skyline is the Macoupin County Courthouse.

Unlike most courthouses of this vintage, the building is still used for its original purpose. In the mid-nineteenth century, it was dubbed the "Million Dollar Courthouse." Residents viewed it as a monument to cronyism and political corruption.

Though the courthouse was not completed at the time, construction was halted in 1870 as costs had exceeded $1.3 million, more the 2,000 percent over budget. At that time, it was the largest courthouse in the United States.

In March 1867, authorization to commence construction was given and the county issued $50,000 in bonds. By January 1869, more than

$449,000 had been spent and the building was still lacking its dome, its roof, and most interior appointments as well as windows. Approval was given for the issuance of additional bonds.

Accusations of fund misappropriations and related legal wrangling became contentious. Judge Thaddeus L. Loomis, a county commissioner, was accused of using stone from the courthouse to build the Loomis House, a hotel, on the nearby square. County Clerk George Holliday was accused of actual theft but left town before charges could be levied. Even with the raising of county taxes to exorbitant levels, the citizens of Macoupin County were unable to pay the debt until 1910.

In addition to the courthouse, E. E. Meyers designed the historic Macoupin County Jail that was completed in 1869. To prevent escapes, cannonballs were inserted into the stone walls, and the cell block's ceiling, walls, and floors were constructed of iron plates. A jailer's residence was built into the upper floors of the parapet. The jail remained in use until 1988. There are plans for renovation that would allow for public tours.

One of the most noticeable buildings on the square is the Loomis House, also designed by architect E. E.

Meyers. It was opened in 1870 as a three-story hotel containing fifty hotel rooms and an expansive dining room. Currently, the location houses several businesses.

Located in front of the United Methodist Church is a large stone monument. It commemorates the spot where Abraham Lincoln delivered a speech on August 31, 1858, during his campaign for United States Senate.

In 1917, the opening of two new coal mines by Standard Oil of Indiana resulted in a severe housing shortage as the town experienced a dramatic growth in population within one year. During this time, from 1908 to 1940, Sears & Roebuck, the mail order sales giant, sold complete kit homes in a variety of styles. Standard Oil officials placed a $1 million order for 156 homes in eight styles. It was the single largest order of houses in Sears history. By the end of 1918, a nine-block neighborhood was complete. With 152 original houses remaining, the Standard Addition in Carlinville is the largest existent collection of these homes.

Established in 1837, Blackburn College has a unique history. In 1864 the school became an accredited four-year college. All classes were open to women.

Dr. William M. Hudson began his tenure as college president in 1912 and the following year introduced the innovative Student "Self Help Plan." Participating students paid $100 tuition and agreed to provide the college with three hours of labor per day. Resultant of this program, Blackburn College is the only college campus in the United States to have been largely built by its students.

Students enrolled in this program learn an array of skills in addition to a liberal arts degree. They work as plumbers, carpenters, painters, janitors, landscapers, cooks, administrative assistants, computer technicians, graphic artists, assistant coaches, tutors, and teaching assistants.

Carlinville, especially along the Route 66 corridor, has a distinct feel of timelessness. Aside from the historic buildings, the Victorian era appearance of the square, and brick-lined streets, this sense is enhanced with businesses such as Taylor's Mexican Chili Company, a restaurant that opened in 1904.

Immediately south of town is the classic CarlinVilla Motel. This renovated historic property is popular with Route 66 travelers.

COLLINSVILLE

Between 1955 and 1957 there was a major realignment of Route 66 in southern Illinois. It was rerouted to the south through Collinsville using Vandalia Avenue, Belt Line Road, and then Collinsville Road into East St. Louis.

Just to the west of Collinsville, on Collinsville Road (Route 66), is Cahokia Mounds State Historic Site, a UNESCO (United Nations Educational, Scientific, and Cultural Organization) World Heritage Site. This is a preserved remnant of a complex of communities that were built on both sides of the Mississippi River around St. Louis and East St. Louis. A staffed interpretive center opened in 1989 and an array of educational programs have been developed for schools.

Within the 2,200-acre (890.3 ha) tract are the central section of one of the most sophisticated native civilizations north of Mexico. This includes a palisade and most of an astronomical site made up of a circle of wooden posts designated "Woodhenge." Archeologists estimate that at its peak in about 1150 CE, Cahokia was larger than London. During this period, the city encompassed an area of at least six miles (9.7 km) and had a population of more than 10,000 people.

The city was dominated by large mounds topped by wooden structures. The mounds along the Mississippi River in this area were once so prevalent that in about 1820, St. Louis was known as Mound City. Monks Mound at Cahokia is one of the largest still existent. At 100 feet (30.5 m) and spanning nearly 14 acres (5.7 ha), Monks Mound is the largest North American prehistoric earthen mound in existence.

In about 1810, John Cook of Shepherdstown, Virginia, built a log cabin at what is now the juncture of Church and Orient Streets in Collinsville. In 1817, Augustus, Anson, and Michael Collins, from Litchfield, Connecticut, purchased Cook's claim. After building another cabin and clearing acreage for a farm, they were joined by their father, mother, brothers, and sisters.

The family established a distillery, grist mill, dairy, and sawmill. As settlers began moving to the area, the Collins family also established a blacksmith shop, wagon works, and related businesses.

MAIN STREET, COLLINSVILLE, ILL.——6

A small village developed around the family's various businesses. It was originally named Downing Station on the post office application filed in November 1819. That application was amended to Unionville in 1822 and again in 1825 as Collinsville. The village was platted in 1837.

There are several historic structures of note in Collinsville. The D. D. Collins House, home of Daniel Dove Collins, was built in 1843 and is listed in the National Register of Historic Places. The First National Bank Building dates to 1887. Still in use is the Collinsville City Hall that was built in 1885. At the time of its construction, the building also housed the post office, library, and the jail.

Built of limestone quarried in Indiana is the State Bank Building built in 1916. The Miner's Institute Building, also known as the Miner's Institute Theater, was built by the local chapter of the coal miners' union in 1918, and the Collinsville Memorial Public Library was built in 1937.

Coal mining in Collinsville commenced in 1870 when Dr. Lumaghi formed a mining company and sank the first shaft. At its peak in about 1920, coal mining, processing, and shipping was the largest employer in Collinsville. Other employers during this period included a lead and zinc foundry, a knitting mill, numerous canning facilities, and factories including one that was the largest producer of cow bells in the country.

In the late 1950s, as US 40 also traversed Collinsville, a small service industry developed. These included some of the earliest of the new chain motel franchises including Howard Johnson's Motor Lodge and Holiday Inn. Independent motels also opened along Collinsville Road including the Rainbo Court Motel and the Round Table Restaurant Motor Lodge.

Counted among unusual landmarks found along the Route 66 corridor between Chicago and Santa Monica is the world's largest catsup bottle in Collinsville. In 1891, the Collinsville Canning and Packing Company was established. In 1907, Elgin and Everett Brooks acquired the company and reorganized it as Triumph Catsup and Pickle Company. Over the course of the next few years, the company was sold several times, but the Brooks brand name was retained as it had acquired an excellent reputation.

By 1940, it was America's leading catsup brand, and in the St. Louis area, it outsold all other brands by a two to one margin. In St. Louis, marketing included the construction of 12-foot (3.7 m)-tall Brooks catsup bottles adorned with neon that slowly rotated. In Sportsman's Park, home of the St. Louis Cardinals and the St. Louis Browns baseball

teams, large banners promoted the catsup.

As part of planned production facility expansion in 1947, the W. E. Caldwell Company of Louisville, Kentucky, was contracted to build a 100,000-gallon (378.5 kl) water tower. It was designed to be built and painted to mimic the company's signature catsup bottle.

In 1995, the Catsup Bottle Preservation Group successfully intervened and prevented demolition of the unique roadside landmark. It was then restored to its original appearance, and in August of 2002, it was added to the National Register of Historic Places.

"HIGHWAY 66 IS THE MAIN MIGRANT ROAD. . . . 66 IS THE PATH OF A PEOPLE IN FLIGHT. . . . 66 IS THE MOTHER ROAD, THE ROAD OF FLIGHT."

—JOHN STEINBECK

CHAPTER TWO

MISSOURI

SHOW-ME STATE

STANTON

In Stanton, Route 66 followed Springfield Road. Largely knit from Native American trade and hunting paths, this was the earliest road between St. Louis and Springfield. Construction was authorized by the State of Missouri in 1837. A few years later, a stage line began providing regularly scheduled service along this route.

In 1857, Congress awarded John Butterfield a contract to establish an overland mail route between the eastern United States and the west coast. The Springfield Road was incorporated into his network.

The following year, the federal government began construction of a telegraph line along the road from St. Louis to Springfield and then south to Fort Smith, Arkansas. During the Civil War, the Springfield Road, or Wire Road, became a vital military corridor that was heavily contested.

Stanton is the successor to the short-lived mining town of Reedville that was located a few miles (5 to 6 km) to the south. A major deposit of copper ore that was developed as the Stanton Copper Mines was the villages cornerstone. It was named

for John Stanton, the financier of the endeavor, a miner, and owner of a powder mill.

On November 11, 1856, a post office application was filed that changed the name from Reedville to Stanton Copper Mines. The town flourished until 1868 when the mines had depleted the ore bodies.

Bennett Thurmond had established a farm with stagecoach stop at the site of present-day Stanton in 1866. In 1868, a town was platted by an investment group and lots sold. The name selected was Stanton, in deference to the mines at Reedville. A post office using this name was established on August 19, 1880.

Meramec Caverns located 3.5 miles (5.6 km) south of Stanton figures prominently in the area's history and the town's association with Route 66. As the largest commercial cavern in the state, it remains a major tourism attraction in Missouri.

Evidence indicates extensive Native American association with the cavern network before arrival of European explorers in the early eighteenth century. Credited with discovery of the cave in the modern

era is given to Philip Renault, a French explorer of the central Mississippi River Valley and surrounding area in 1719.

Renault was sent into the Meramec Valley by the Mississippi Company of Kaskaskia to develop recently discovered deposits of lead in the 1720s. This is most likely when he discovered Meramec Caverns.

After the withdrawal of the French, Spanish explorers and miners moved into the area. In 1760, a mining party led by Don Serita Gonzales began using the caverns as their base of operations for lead and copper mining in the area. The copper mines were eventually abandoned but were reactivated in the mid-nineteenth century by John Stanton.

The caverns were also used for the mining of saltpeter and the manufacture of gunpowder. This enterprise gave the cavern its original name, Saltpeter Cave. It was renamed Meramec Caverns by Lester B. Dill.

Gunpowder mills are an integral part of the cavern's modern history. The challenge, however, is in separating fact from fiction. A primary element of promotional literature for the caverns as a tourist attraction has been the embellishment of history and local legend.

As an example, in a brochure produced in 1971, it was noted that, "Very little exploration was done until 1862–1864, during the Civil War, when gunpowder manufacturing was at its height at the

DANCEING IN MERAMEC CAVE
STANTON MO, U.S. HY 66.

cave. The Union forces set up powder kilns and leaching vats in the cavern, as well as an underground railroad station. Thousands of slaves found freedom via this route."

However, brochures published in 1955 and 1942 do not mention the Underground Railroad. And the first mention of an association with Jesse James was in materials produced during the mid-1940s.

After the cave's acquisition by Charles Ruepple in 1898, a large dance floor was built in the room at the entrance of the caverns. This made Stanton and the caverns a popular attraction for people from as far away as St. Louis.

After master promoter Lester Dill purchased the caverns in 1933, the site was transformed into a major destination. He had a modern road built to the caverns and the former dance hall converted into a cool parking area.

Local children were hired to wire carboard caverns promotions to car bumpers. Emulating the successful Lookout Mountain's Rock City Gardens "SEE ROCK CITY" painted barn advertisements, Dill had the caverns similarly promoted along Route 66.

When artifacts were found during cavern explorations in 1941, Dill linked them to the local legend that Frank and Jesse James had used the caverns as a hideout. Building on the legend, in 1949, Dill built a cabin near the entrance and relocated J. Frank Dalton from Oklahoma. The one-hundred-year-old Dalton had made news with the claim that he was Jesse James.

He further magnified this promotion by purchasing an old log cabin, dismantling it, and having it rebuilt deep in the cavern. He then claimed it was Jesse James hideout.

This was but one of many successful and innovative promotional campaigns that made the caverns a popular destination for Route 66 travelers. The scenic beauty of the cave system, its association with Route 66, and the blurring of history have ensured that Meramec caverns remains a popular attraction.

The town of Stanton capitalized on its proximity to the caverns. Motels and quirky roadside attractions such as the Jesse James Wax Museum thrived as traffic along Route 66 increased in the postwar years.

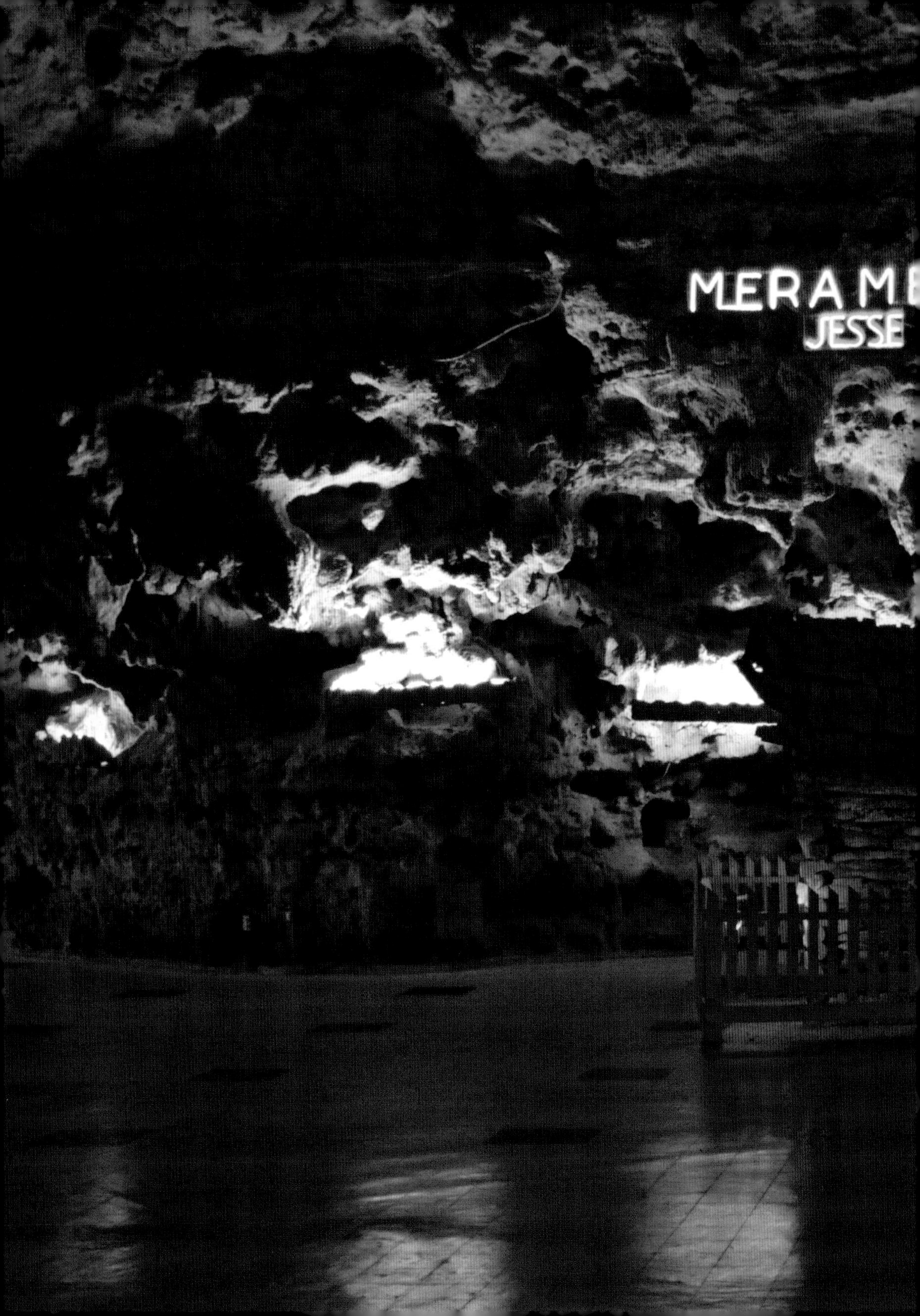
MERAME
JESSE

CAVERNS
HIDEOUT
ES

MERAMEC CAVERNS
"The 4-Story Wonder"   STANTON, MO.

MISSOURI'S LARGEST ELECTRIC LIGHTED CAVE
. . . World's only drive-in cave. Room for 300 cars.

CUBA

In Cuba, US 66 coursed through town on Washington Boulevard. This was but one block north of Main Street.

There is relative certainty that this Ozark Mountains village was named after the Caribbean Island of the same name. The reason, however, is a matter of conjecture.

Among Route 66 enthusiasts, Cuba is best known for the Wagon Wheel Motel. This is the longest continuously operated motel on Route 66 and an icon in the era of that highway's renaissance. Dating to 1935, this renovated motel was listed on the National Register of Historic Places in 2003.

The 1940 *Directory of Motor Courts and Cottages* published by AAA described the motel as, "10 new, well built stone cottages, each with private tub or shower bath, hot and cold running water. Well furnished and maintained. This is a home away from home." For more than fifteen years, the property was given a AAA recommendation.

The time capsule feel of Cuba is made manifest in the historic business district, along the Route 66

corridor, on Main Street and on State Highway 19. An example of this is the 19 Drive-In that opened on highway 19 in June 1955.

On Main Street are two former railroad hotels that have been converted into apartment buildings. Dating to the teens, the Hotel Cuba and Southern Hotel were built across from the train depot that has been razed. In 1931, to capitalize on Route 66 traffic, the Hotel Cuba built a new portico and entrance at the rear of the hotel that faced the highway.

The Southern Hotel has an association with the actress Bette Davis through a comedic incident that occurred in 1948. Davis and her driver stopped at the hotel for dinner during a trip west on Route 66. Wilbur Vaughn, a nineteen-year-old man that worked at the theater located a block from the hotel, recognized the actress and asked if he could take her photograph. The request was denied.

In an interview Vaughn said, "It was a cold, rainy Monday night, and I waited outside the Southern Hotel until Miss Davis came out. I then snapped a photo which he had been forbidden to take earlier

in the evening by Miss Davis's male companion. The companion was so angered that he chased me down the street, cursing all the way. I dodged behind a gas station and heard a 'thump' behind me. The man was face down in the mud. I ran to the theater."

The photo was printed in the *Cuba News & Review* the following week. The incident has been commemorated in a mural painted by artist Ray Harvey on the Cuba Free Press building.

Throughout the community are colorful murals that illustrate incidents in the city's history. This has led to Cuba being proclaimed Missouri's Mural City. One of these murals illustrates another celebrity association with Cuba.

A feature published in the *Muskogee Times-Democrat* on September 4, 1928, tells the story of Amelia Earhart's emergency landing outside of Cuba during a flight from Scott Field in Belleville, Illinois, to Los Angeles in a 1927 Avro Avian airplane. The article notes that there was minimal damage to the aircraft and that Earhart was not injured.

A series of murals chronicle the battles between the troops of Confederate General Sterling Price and Union General Thomas Ewing in September 1864. The battle commenced with an assault on the armory and ammunition dump at Fort Davidson in Pilot Knob, Missouri, near Cuba. Ewing's retreat is illustrated in two panels. Another panel represents Price's destruction of the depot and train tracks in Cuba in an attempt to thwart Ewing's escape.

Cuba is an unlikely location for an unusual attraction: shoes that once belonged to Robert Wadlow, the Gentle Giant from Alton, Illinois. During the 1930s, Wadlow was billed as the world's tallest man. He stood 8 feet 11.1 inches (2.7 m) tall and weighed an astonishing 490 pounds (222.3 kg).

At age 20, Wadlow signed a contract with the International Shoe Company. In exchange for free, custom-made shoes, he traveled the country on a promotional tour representing the company. His used shoes were sold to shoe stores as promotional items.

Henry Hayes, the original owner of Hayes Shoe Store in Cuba, and his wife Audrey acquired the first shoe when they purchased the store in 1950. It was a size 35AA. Several years later, the International Shoe Company launched a unique promotional campaign. One of Wadlow's shoes was loaned to the shoe store. It was filled with shelled corn. To win a free pair of shoes, customers had to guess the number of kernels.

At the end of the promotion, store owners had the option of purchasing the shoe. Hayes chose to buy the size 37AA shoe. As a result, this became one of the few stores in the country to have two of the Alton Giant's shoes.

Located south of town is Maramec Spring Park. This is a stunning scenic wonder that centers on a flooded cavern and a spring that flows with 100 million gallons (378,541.2 kl) of fresh water per day. The park also contains the expansive and picturesque ruins of the Maramec Iron Works established in 1826.

WAYNESVILLE

In Waynesville, Route 66 followed a direct line through the heart of the town. Today, this route is signed as State Highway 17 and Business 44.

The namesake for Waynesville is General Anthony Wayne, an American Revolutionary War hero dubbed "Mad Anthony" for his disregard for personal safety during the Battle of Stony Point.

A trading post was established along the banks of Roubidoux Creek in about 1833. A post office application was filed in 1834.

The creek figures prominently in the city's history. Today, it is also the focal point for Laughlin Park, a blending of historic sites and nature preserve, and Roubidoux Creek Conservation Area.

Laughlin Park is one of the only Nationally Certified Historic Sites along the Trail of Tears. In 1830, President Andrew Jackson signed the Indian Removal Act. This gave the federal government the power to exchange Native American tribal lands in the southern Mississippi River Valley and in southeast states for land to the west in an area designated the "Indian colonization zone." The relocation of tribes to the Indian Territory became known collectively as the Trail of Tears.

U.S. HIGHWAY 66 WAYNESVILLE MO. IN THE OZARKS.

On June 19, 2015, seven Trail of Tears Wayside Exhibits were unveiled at Roubidoux Spring in the park. The unveiling event marked another step in the National Park Service's effort to preserve related sites and develop increased public awareness of the trail's significance. The interpretive walking trail along the creek and through the nature preserve includes seven detailed wayside kiosks, including a description of the site of a Cherokee removal campsite and the Trail of Tears crossing.

Another location that has an association with Waynesville's early history is the Old Stagecoach Stop that was originally known as Waynesville House built in 1854 or 1855. Today, it is a ten-room museum. Each room is used for displays that highlight a specific era in the building's history.

It has served as a stagecoach stop, inn, and tavern on the Wire Road that connected St. Louis and Springfield. It was used as a hospital during the Civil War. It has also served as a boarding house and provided housing for workers building Fort Leonard Wood in 1941.

The Wire Road was a strategic military corridor during the Civil War. A fort was established on the bluff above town by the Union Army to protect the road and to serve as a supply depot.

The Talbot House is another historic building of significance. It was built in 1885 by Reverend Albert

Washington Davis, the pastor of Waynesville Methodist Church. He died in 1888 at the age of 26. His widow turned the house into a hotel. It was purchased by Dr. Charles A. Talbot in March 1920. After a period of vacancy in the 1990s, the house was purchased and restored in 2001 and became Talbot House Antiques, Collectables & Gifts. As of early 2021 it was listed as permanently closed.

Waynesville was designated the Pulaski County seat. The first courthouse was a log structure built in just two weeks in 1839. A larger courthouse was built four years later. During the Civil War, this building served as a hospital for the Union Army.

The third courthouse was built in 1872 for a cost of $8,000. Built of brick, the two-story structure burned in 1903 after being struck by lightning.

Its replacement built in 1903 served as a courthouse until 1990. It was listed in the National Register of Historic Places in 1979.

The Pulaski County Courthouse now houses a museum with exhibits chronicling the city's history through the Civil War, World War I, World War II, and Desert Storm. At this historic building in 1990, Governor John Ashcroft signed legislation that designated the 307 miles (494 km) of Route 66 in Missouri as a historic byway.

WAYNESVILLE BRIDGE SHOWING BELL HOTEL IN BACKGROUND, ON U. S. HIGHWAY 66, WAYNESVILLE, MO.

A tangible link to the city's connection to Route 66 is the renovated Roubidoux Bridge. Built in 1923, this concrete arch bridge was a component in an improvement project for State Highway 14. It was designed by the Missouri State Highway Commission and built by Koss Construction Company at the cost of $44,035. It was widened in 1939 to accommodate a sidewalk for pedestrians. Today it is the last bridge of its type in Missouri.

Until Fort Leonard Wood construction commenced, agricultural, tourism, and a service industry fueled the economy. *The WPA to Missouri Guide* (Works Progress Administration) published in 1941 noted that Waynesville had a "leisurely atmosphere, unmarred by the smoke of industry. . . ."

Jack Rittenhouse, in *A Guide Book to Highway 66*, alluded to the dramatic transformation of the town during World War II resultant of establishment of nearby Fort Leonard Wood as a primary training center for the United States Army. This military installation continues to be an important component of the local economy.

Realignment of Route 66 to the south of town as a four-lane highway, the current course of I-44, during the 1940s further transformed the town, leaving the original path of the highway as City 66. The core of the old business district along this corridor has been revived as a vibrant arts and dining district.

Popular with Route 66 travelers, especially those from Europe, locals, and personnel stationed at Fort Leonard Wood, is Paradise Deli. For more than forty years, this restaurant has specialized in authentic German cuisine. They also sell European groceries.

CARTHAGE

Route 66 in Carthage followed several different roads through town due to realignment. But regardless of alignment, the skyline was dominated by the imposing Jasper County Courthouse built in 1895. Listed on the National Register of Historic Places in 1973, this architectural masterpiece is recognized as the second-most photographed manmade site in the state of Missouri.

Surrounding the courthouse square are an array of businesses and storefronts in buildings that date to the mid-nineteenth century. The diverse array of unaltered architectural styles resulted in the district's listing in the National Register of Historic Places in 1980.

Jasper County was named for Revolutionary War hero William Jasper and established on January 29, 1841. Designation of Carthage as the county seat was pronounced on March 28, 1842.

An interesting aspect of the courthouse square is the array of monuments and memorials commemorating key moments in the city's history such as the Osage War. Farming in the area commenced in the area after the Osage tribes were relocated to the Indian Territories in what is now Oklahoma during the 1830s. In 1837, bands of Osage returned in search of lands for farming and hunting. Governor Lilburn Boggs issued orders for the

BOOT'S CAFE
CARTHAGE, MO.

state militia to remove the Osage and return them to lands allocated in treaties.

Another monument details the Battle of Carthage that commenced on July 5, 1861. This was the first of thirteen Civil War battles that centered on Carthage. In the final battle on September 22, 1864, Confederate forces put most of the city to the torch.

Myra Maybelle "Belle" Shirley, later known as Belle Starr after marrying Sam Starr, leader of an outlaw gang based in the Indian Territory, was born on Feb. 5, 1848, near Carthage, Missouri. Their farm was a haven for fugitives such as Frank and Jesse James. Starr was shot and killed in 1889. Her shooting remains unsolved.

Although historical evidence is scant, her exploits earned her a reputation as "the Bandit Queen." Actress Gene Tierney played the lead role in a film entitled *Belle Starr* released in 1941. Noted western biographer Glenn Shirley chronicled her story in *Belle Starr and Her Times: The Literature, the Facts, and the Legends*.

In 1930, in national headlines, Carthage was linked to another criminal. On December 13, Eli Othel Bray, a jailer with the Carthage Police Department, was overwhelmed and killed with his service revolver. Under the pretense of visiting a prisoner, 18-year-old Wilbur Henson and his 20-year-old wife attacked Bray during an aborted jail break.

They fled west on US 66 and were arrested near Chelsea, Oklahoma. After being convicted of Bray's murder, Henson escaped from the Missouri State penitentiary. He remained at large for four years until he was eventually captured in Los Angeles, California.

In the post–Civil War years, Carthage developed with a richly diverse economy. Aside from agriculture, the city was a railroad and industrial town. Mining also fueled prosperity as the city was centered in an area of rich deposits of lead, and there were quarries for extraction of quality marble and limestone.

The gray marble from Carthage quarries was used in an array of national construction projects. These included the Missouri State Capitol, the United States Capitol, and the White House.

In the early twentieth century, the town's economy was further diversified with the establishment of service industries. Growth of this sector was fueled by the increasing flow of traffic as Carthage was a crossroads for the Jefferson Highway that connected New Orleans, Louisiana, to Winnipeg, Manitoba, Canada, and the Ozark Trails Highway that connected St. Louis, Missouri, with Las Vegas, New Mexico. With the designation of Route 66 in 1926, there was an exponential growth in traffic and a corresponding growth in the service industry.

Jack Rittenhouse's *A Guide Book to Highway 66* contains entries about the legend of Belle Starr and the Battle of Carthage. It also lists three hotels, cabins, and garages.

The most notable vestiges of the town's association with Route 66 are Boots Court, Boots Drive-In built across the street, and the 66 Drive-In Theater. Arthur Boots built the motel in 1939. A recent renovation has restored the property to its 1940s appearance. Even though it retains many original features, Boots Drive-In has been modified to serve various businesses including a real estate office and credit union.

In 1940, Clark Gable was purportedly a guest at the hotel and stayed in room number six. Local legend also claims that Gene Autry and Smiley Burnett were guests.

The 66 Drive-In Theater established by V. F. Naramore and W.D. Bradfield opened on September 22, 1949. The first showing was *Two Guys from Texas*. It remained operational until 1985 at which time the site was used by a salvage yard. After refurbishment, it reopened as a theater on April 3, 1997.

During the 2013 Route 66 International Festival, the theater hosted a special showing of the animated film *Cars*, complete with an appearance by Michael Wallis, the voice of the character Sheriff. Indicative of the international nature of Route 66 in the twenty-first century, in attendance was a Route 66 Germany tour.

CHAPTER THREE

KANSAS

SUNFLOWER STATE

GALENA

During its history, Route 66 followed several courses through the heart of Galena. Streets used include East Front Street, North and South Main Street, and 7th Street.

The name for the community is derived from the type of lead ore that spurred expansive development of mines in the tristate area. Before 1877, this was an agricultural area of scattered farms.

In that year, two Joplin miners, John Shoe and John McAllen, were prospecting in Cherokee County, Kansas. Along Short Creek, they discovered lead deposits. Then, after acquiring permission from landowner

J. Nichols, they dug a shaft and struck a rich vein of lead just fifteen feet (4.6 m) below the surface.

Miners and speculators flooded the area. Land prices soared. Nichol's 120-acre (48.6 ha) farm appraised at three dollars an acre (0.4 ha) before the discovery was sold to the West Joplin Lead & Zinc Company for $7,000. Mining companies began buying large tracts of land. Sections were platted as townsites on both sides of Short Creek.

In May 1877, Galena was incorporated on land owned by the South Side Town & Mining Company. Empire City was incorporated in

June 1877 opposite Galena on land owned by the Murphy Mining Company. Both towns boomed as new discoveries were made, fueling the growth of the mines. There is evidence that the town of Galena had a population of nearly 3,000 people by the end of the first summer. Empire City had a similar population and a post office by July.

The rivalry between the communities was intense and occasionally violent. On July 25, to curb growth in Galena, the Empire City Council authorized construction of a stockade of heavy timbers along the border between the communities. This would curtail stagecoach service, freight deliveries, and even United States mail service to Galena and Baxter Springs as a large detour would be required.

Threats, intimidation, and physical assaults on the men building the fence led to Empire City authorizing police protection. Mayor George Webb of Galena petitioned state and federal governments to intervene.

When these appeals failed, Webb, with approval of the Galena council, deputized a posse of 50 men who arrested workers attempting to close the road. Then, early on the morning of August 15, Webb's posse torched the wall. After authorization, a deputy in Empire City arrested Webb

in Galena for arson. He was taken to Empire City tried and convicted. On appeal, he was acquitted.

The wall was never rebuilt. Controversies between the two communities continued and were contested in the courts. It was not until July 9, 1907, that Empire City was incorporated into Galena.

There is an obscure celebrity association with Galena. In January 1898, Harry Houdini made his debut as a "Spiritualist" in the city's opera house.

During World War I, the mines in the tristate area were among the largest producers of lead and zinc in the world. As a result, from the teens through the immediate postwar years of the 1940s, Galena remained prosperous with a population that neared 15,000. The downward spiral for Galena was fueled by the closure of the mines and the replacement of Route 66 with I-44 that resulted in Kansas being the only state associated with Route 66 completely bypassed. In the census of 2000, the population was listed as less than 4,000.

Just to the east of Galena along Route 66 is the site of the Eagle Picher Company, a smelter that was the focus of one of the most violent labor disputes during the 1930s. The disputes reached a fever pitch when

Eagle Pisher Lead Smelter Galena, Kan.
Paul Osborn, Artist.

in 1935, John L. Lewis, president of the United Mine Workers, called a labor strike against this facility.

The company responded by bringing in non-union workers from Missouri, Kansas, and Oklahoma via Route 66. Angry miners responded by barricading US 66, forcing sheriff deputies to detour traffic into Galena.

As the violence escalated, Governor Alf Landon declared martial law and dispatched National Guard troops to Galena. On April 11, 1937, more than four thousand men armed with pick handles stormed the headquarters of the International Mine, Mill, and Smelter Workers Union in protest of organization efforts. The demonstration culminated with nine men shot to death in front of the union headquarters in Galena.

The city's colorful history and an array of mineral specimens are on display at the Galena Mining & Historical Museum. The museum is housed in the former Missouri-Kansas-Texas train depot.

An old Kan-O-Tex service station at the north end of Main Street was the cornerstone for revitalization built on renewed interest in Route 66. Renovated and converted into a souvenir shop by Betty Courtney, Melba Rigg, Renee Charles, and Judy Courtney, the renamed 4 Women on The Route became a popular stop for Route 66 travelers.

Immediately to the south of Galena is the Schermerhorn Park and Southeast Kansas Nature Center, home to some of the rarest animals in Kansas including species of fish, salamanders, and mussels. The park was established in 1922 and was a popular stop for Route 66 travelers. The picturesque stone walls, terraces, and structures were built in the 1930s as a Works Progressive Administration (WPA) project.

BAXTER SPRINGS

Baxter Springs was one of the first settlements in Cherokee County. It was named for John L. Baxter who settled at a mineral spring near the present townsite in 1849. Prior to Baxter's arrival, the spring on the Black Dog Trail was revered by Native Americans as a place of healing.

Baxter built an inn and store at the site to capitalize on traffic along the military road that connected Fort Scott, Fort Leavenworth, and Fort Gibson. A section of this historic road is signed today as Military Avenue. This was the course of Route 66 in Baxter Springs.

In 1857, a military encampment was established near the springs to provide a base for Colonel Joseph Johnson's survey parties that were establishing the boundary between Kansas and Indian Territory. During the Civil War, a small military outpost named Fort Blair was established at present day Baxter Springs. This encampment was garrisoned by the 2nd Kansas Colored Infantry and was supplemented by a regiment of cavalry from Wisconsin.

On October 6, 1863, a band of Confederate guerrillas led by William Quantrill attacked Fort

Main Street, Baxter Springs, Kansas

Blair after routing a Union patrol. Even though they were heavily outnumbered, the troops at the fort repulsed several attacks.

First Lieutenant James Burton Pond received the Medal of Honor for leading the defense of the fort. The citation for his Medal of Honor reads: "For extraordinary heroism on 6 October 1863, while serving with Company C, 3d Wisconsin Cavalry, in action at Baxter Springs, Kansas. While in command of two companies of Cavalry, First Lieutenant Pond was surprised and attacked by several times his own number of guerrillas, but gallantly rallied his men, and after a severe struggle drove the enemy outside the fortifications. First Lieutenant Pond then went outside the works and, alone and unaided, fired a howitzer three times, throwing the enemy into confusion and causing him to retire."

After being repelled, Quantrill's raiders encountered General James Blunt and his entourage leading a supply column and relocating his headquarters from Fort Scott to Fort Smith, Arkansas. The incident that is today known as the Baxter Springs Massacre was a vicious but short battle. The raiders overpowered and scattered the column and began hunting down survivors in the ravines and gullies. A patrol

from Fort Blair later reported that the massacre site covered several square miles (18 km2).

In 1868, the year that the town of Baxter Springs was incorporated, an acre (0.4 ha) of land in the center of the new city cemetery was deeded to the government. The soldiers who died in the battle and massacre had been buried north of the fort in a common grave immediately following the disaster. Their bodies were exhumed and interred in the Baxter Springs City Cemetery Soldier's Lot that year.

In 1885, an imposing marker was placed in the center of the plot by The Daughters of the American Revolution. The marker is inscribed with the names of those known to have died on October 6, 1863. This is one stop on a self-guided driving tour to sites associated with the battle and massacre. The map and brochure are available at the Baxter Springs Heritage Center, which houses an extensive collection of Civil War artifacts.

After cessation of hostilities, Baxter Springs figured prominently in the development of the western cattle industry. Commencing in 1866, herds of longhorn cattle were driven from central Texas to Baxter Springs over the Eastern Shawnee Trail

where brokers negotiated for the cows. With completion of a rail line from Kansas City to Baxter Springs in 1870, the town boomed.

As with many frontier communities, the town developed a reputation for violence during its infancy. However, the incidents involving Marshall Seaman and Marshal C.M. Taylor were unique.

On November 7, 1870, Marshall Seaman was called to the Wiggins House to settle a dispute between A. Wiggins, proprietor, Isham Good, a cowboy from Texas, and Nellie Starr, noted as a woman of ill repute in the court proceedings. As he attempted to arrest Starr, she and Good opened fire. The marshal was mortally wounded in the crossfire. Wiggins would recover from his injuries.

For reasons unknown, only Good was accused of murder. After being released on bail, he fled to the Indian Territory. Starr was charged with violent and indecent behavior and disorderly conduct. After paying the required fines, she resumed her business activities at the Wiggins House.

The city council appointed C. M. Taylor to replace the late marshal.

In June of 1872, Taylor was ordered to serve a warrant on J. R. Boyd, the mayor of Baxter Springs. A Galena, Kansas, merchant had filed a claim against the mayor for repayment of debt.

When the marshal attempted to arrest the mayor, an argument ensued. Boyd pulled a revolver and shot the marshal. The sheriff promptly arrested Mayor Boyd for murder. Released on bail, he continued in his duties as mayor until being acquitted of the charge of murder, claiming self-defense.

From the mid-1880s through the 1950s, Baxter Springs figured prominently as a bustling, progressive mining town. The town was located at the center of a vast lead and zinc mining district that included the southeast corner of Kansas and the communities in southwest Missouri and northeast Oklahoma. During the years bracketing World War I, this area was the largest producer of lead in the world.

The Baxter Springs Visitor Center is housed in a renovated Independent Oil and Gas Company station that opened on July 7, 1930. The building was listed on the National Register of Historic Places in 2003.

"LIFE IS EITHER A DARING ADVENTURE OR NOTHING."

—HELEN KELLER

CHAPTER FOUR

OKLAHOMA

SOONER STATE

COMMERCE

The initial alignment of Route 66 followed Main Street and Commerce Street. It was later rerouted onto Mickey Mantle Boulevard. This is now the course for US 69.

This was one of the last towns established in the tristate mining district that was the largest producer of lead and zinc in the world during the years bracketing World War I. The first ore discoveries and earliest mining operations in Ottawa County, Oklahoma, occurred in the vicinity of Peoria in 1891. The next major ore discoveries occurred northeast of Lincolnville near Quapaw in 1902, followed by discoveries in 1905 near Commerce.

A boom in zinc and lead mining began in the area after a major ore discovery in 1914 near the current location of Picher, Oklahoma.

During the peak of mining activities in the mid-1920s, an average of 130,410 tons (118,306 t) of lead and 749,254 tons (679,711 t) of zinc were being produced annually. According to records maintained by the Bureau of Mines, a total of 181,048,872 tons (164,244,774 t) of crude ore were produced from the Oklahoma portion of the district.

Commerce was first platted as Hattonville, named after Amos Hatton who had developed the Emma Gordon mine in 1906. However, the initial post office application filed in 1913 used the name North Miami. In June 1914, this was amended, and the name become Commerce. The name was derived from the Commerce Mining and Royalty Company that operated the largest mine in the area.

An early investor in Commerce mines was Harry S. Truman. With Thomas Hughes, Jerry Culbertson, and an uncle as partners, and money advanced by his mother, in 1915, Truman acquired controlling interest in the Eureka Mine. The partners then formed the T.C.H. Mining Company.

The town was developed on lands that had been assigned to the Quapaw by the federal government. In 1834, the federal government relocated the tribe to the Indian Territory west of the current Missouri state line.

Indicative of the town's rapid growth, in late 1908, the Oklahoma, Kansas & Missouri Interurban Railway built a line connecting Commerce to Miami, another mining town a few miles (5 to 6 km) to the south. In 1921, an extensive electrified trolley system was established for mine workers.

In 1918, the town boasted two banks, two theaters, two modern hotels, two newspapers, and a diverse business district. The 1920 population stood at 2,555.

Mining remained the primary foundation for the town's economy through the late 1950s. After decades of transitioning to an agricultural base, Commerce received an economic boost when the Environmental Protection Agency's Superfund Site program began cleaning up decades of toxic lead mining waste.

As evidenced by Mickey Mantle Boulevard, Mickey Mantle is Commerce's most famous resident. Related sites include Mutt Mantle Field named for his father. His boyhood home, a private residence, is at 319 S. Quincy. His professional career was launched when he was hired by the minor league Baxter Springs Whiz Kids in Baxter Springs, Kansas.

In 2010, Commerce honored Mantle by unveiling a 9-foot (2.7 m) bronze statue. It stands just beyond the center field wall of Mickey Mantle Field at 400 S. Mickey Mantle Boulevard. It can be seen from Route 66.

As with many communities in this part of Oklahoma, Commerce has a connection with Bonnie and Clyde. On Friday, April 6, 1934, just south of US 66 near Commerce, their stolen 1934 Ford became mired in mud. An attempt to commandeer a vehicle at gunpoint on the New State Road failed, and the motorist who escaped notified police in Commerce.

Police Chief Percy Boyd and Constable Cal Campbell responded. When Campbell and Boyd arrived on the scene, they were immediately fired upon. In the exchange of gunfire, sixty-year-old Campbell, a single

Allen's Fillin' Station

CONOCO

Built in 1929-1930 by F.D. Mitchell

FULL SERVICE

CONOCO

REGULAR

CONOCO

Allens Fillin Station

We Fix
Flyin
Saucers

Corner Of Okla. U.S. 44 Commerce

father of eight, was struck in the heart and killed. Boyd received a minor head wound and was forced to surrender.

Leaving the body of Campbell in the mud by the roadside, the outlaws drove north with Chief Boyd as a hostage. He was later released nine miles (14.5 km) south of Fort Scott, Kansas. Campbell became the first Ottawa County lawman to die while on duty. A monument commemorating Campbell is near the police department.

In *A Guide Book to Highway 66*, Jack Rittenhouse noted the only auto court in Commerce was O'Brien's Camp. He also noted that it was a time of "limited facilities" and listed one garage, Sult's, and mineral specimen shop located "where US 66 makes a sharp turn." The *AAA Directory of Motor Courts and Cottages* for 1940 also lists O'Brien's Camp as the only auto court with the message that fourteen units had running water. Four units that did not have water rented for $1.00 per night.

For Route 66 enthusiasts, a destination is the Dairy King. Housed in a circa 1927 Marathon service station, this old-fashioned burger stand is world renowned for its handmade Route 66 shield shaped cookies.

A unique time capsule is Allen's Conoco Fillin' Station. Established in 1929 or 1930 by F.D. Mitchell, the cottage-style station was built against the wall of the building behind it presenting an interesting optical illusion.

CLAREMORE

Route 66 followed J. M. Davis Boulevard, which was also the course of the Ozark Trails Highway. US 66 also followed Lynn Riggs Boulevard from 1948 to 1985. The latter is now signed as State Highway 66.

The county seat of Rogers County, Claremore, is named for Osage chief Claremore, whose nearby village was destroyed during the Battle of Claremore Mound in 1817. The exact date of the town's founding is a matter of conjecture.

The railroad figures prominently in the city's early history. The Atlantic & Pacific Railroad reached the townsite in 1882, and the Kansas & Arkansas Valley Railway arrived in 1889. Claremore's importance as a transportation hub would continue into the twentieth century since the town was located on the Ozark Trails, a network of early automobile roads, and later, US 66 as well as State Highways 20, 66, and 88.

The search for oil led to an unexpected discovery that transformed the town. In 1903, George Eaton, owner of a small oil company, sank an exploratory well and unleashed an artesian flow of mineral waters that were proclaimed to be rich with radium. For centuries, these types of waters were deemed recuperative for an array of ailments, so numerous entrepreneurs hoping to capitalize on the waters established bath houses. Humorist Will Rogers joked that the water would "cure you of everything but being a Democrat."

The hotels and bath houses quickly became Claremore's biggest industry, and by the early 1930s, the city was a destination for legions of visitors that arrived via Route 66 or the railroad. People from Tulsa and Oklahoma City, Joplin, and other area communities would often travel to Claremore for a weekend. Out-of-state visitors would stay for a week or more.

The Claremore Chamber of Commerce devised an array of marketing and promotional campaigns. One of the most novel was Bath Week. As per arrangement with bathhouse and resort owners, a percentage of bath ticket sales would be allocated to the chamber of commerce for the promotion of Claremore and its radium water springs.

As the event evolved, an expansive parade complete with bands and floats was added to the festivities. Of Bath Week, Will Rogers once quipped, "We have all kinds of various 'weeks.' 'Eat an apple week.'

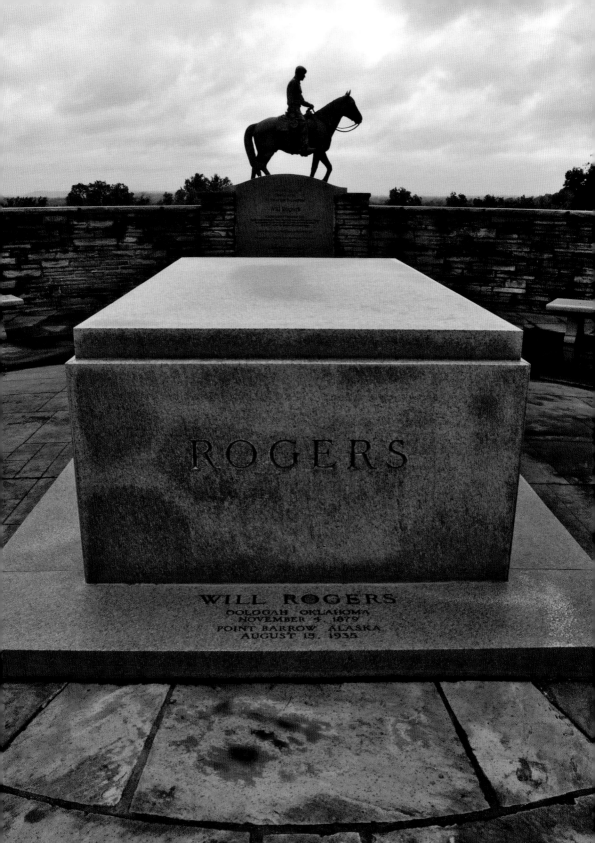

ROGERS

WILL ROGERS
OOLOGAH OKLAHOMA
NOVEMBER 4, 1879
POINT BARROW ALASKA
AUGUST 15, 1935

'Don't shoot your husband week.' 'Don't cuss the Republicans any more than you can help week.' But Claremore, the home of the great radium water, is having this week one of the most practical and useful ones, 'Take a bath week.' Even the Rotarys, Kiwanis, Lions, Apes, and Chamber of Commerce have joined in the novelty of the thing."

Will Rogers spent some years of his boyhood in Claremore and in 1911 purchased 20 acres (8.1 ha) on a hill overlooking the town. This is now the site of the Will Rogers Memorial Museum. The museum houses an array of artifacts including memorabilia, photographs, and manuscripts. Movies starring Rogers are shown in a theater.

Will Rogers was originally buried in California. In 1944, shortly after

completion of a new sunken garden built in front of the memorial to Rogers, his body was interred in Claremore. His wife Betty was also buried in the tomb.

To capitalize on the international notoriety of Will Rogers and the popularity of the waters, Louis Abraham, Walter Krumrei, and Morton Harrison partnered to build the Hotel Will Rogers. Located on Will Rogers Boulevard, the hotel and resort opened with a gala celebration on February 7, 1930. Built at a cost of $321,000, the six-story, 78-room hotel with Spanish decor and furnishings quickly earned a reputation as a destination for the rich and famous.

By the 1980s, the hotel had faded from prominence. It was closed in 1991. Deemed a blight on the

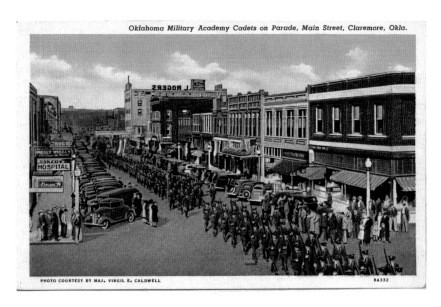

Oklahoma Military Academy Cadets on Parade, Main Street, Claremore, Okla.

PHOTO COURTESY BY MAJ. VIRGIL E. CALDWELL   8A332

community, plans were made for demolition. But in 1994, the Rogers County Historical Society purchased the historic hotel to save it from destruction. It underwent renovation and reopened in 1997 as The Will Rogers Center, an apartment complex for seniors.

Will Rogers is not the only celebrity associated with Claremore. Singer Patti Page, astronaut Stuart Roosa, and Lynn Riggs, author of *Green Grows the Lilacs*, from which the musical *Oklahoma!* was adapted, are natives of the city.

Claremore is also home to the J. M. Davis Arms & Historical Museum, the world's largest collection of historic firearms. In Jack Rittenhouse's *A Guide Book to Highway 66*, it is noted that, "In the Mason Hotel lobby is a collection of 6,000 guns—the largest individual gun collection in the world, assembled by J.M. Davis including weapons of Emmett Dalton, Pancho Villa, Henry Starr, Cole Younger, Pretty Boy Floyd, and others, as well as several ancient pieces."

Davis donated the collection to the state of Oklahoma in 1969. This became the nucleus for the expansive museum that also contains guns and small artillery pieces from the fourteenth century through the mid-twentieth century. There are also exhibits of nineteenth-century music boxes, a diverse array of American Indian relics, vintage music instruments, John Wayne memorabilia, and World War I recruitment posters.

A rare vestige of prewar Route 66 is the Adobe Village Apartments. The 1940 AAA *Directory of Motor Courts and Cottages* lists this complex as El Sueno Courts.

COFFEE SHOP

MASON HOTEL COFFEE SHOP, CLAREMORE, OKLAHOMA

STROUD

Route 66 followed Main Street through Stroud. This is now designated State Highway 66. To the east of town, the original alignment of the highway is signed as Old US 66.

In 1892, James Wrexel Stroud built a store, trading post, and post office on his homestead six miles (9.7 km) from the Sac and Fox Indian Agency. This was one mile (1.6 km) west of the present townsite. Stroud had carefully selected the site because the sale of alcohol was permitted at his site.

The town was doing quite well when the St. Louis–San Francisco Railroad, also called the Frisco Railroad, began construction of a line between Sapulpa and Oklahoma City that would bypass Stroud by a mile (1.6 km). So, Stroud bought land one mile (1.6 km) east of the town and sold a right-of-way to the railroad company. Then in 1898, he sold most of the remaining land to Luther F. Aldrich, a town developer.

Some residents were reluctant to move from already developed land in "old Stroud" to the new location. Those who moved razed buildings and rebuilt in "new Stroud." Transition from a frontier to modern community began when the first train pulled into Stroud on August 17, 1898.

Saloons and the sale of liquor provided a substantial part of city revenue. As Oklahoma was admitted into the union as a dry state in 1907, prohibition dealt the community a harsh blow. As a result, cotton farming became important. By 1909, Stroud was a prosperous community with two newspapers, banks, cotton gins, and a mill for cottonseed oil.

With establishment of the Ozark Trail Highway to connect St. Louis, Missouri, to Las Vegas, New Mexico, in 1913, the economy in Stroud was diversified with development of a service industry catering to the need of automobilists. A few miles (5 to 6 km) west of Stroud at the intersection of two county farm roads stands a 21-foot (6.4 m) obelisk built as a directional marker on the Ozark Trail Highway. A study found that only seven of these markers are still existent.

In 1915, an incident that some historians see as the last chapter of the frontier era in Oklahoma placed Stroud in banner headlines throughout the country. The attempt at a double bank robbery would not have been overly noteworthy if Henry Starr had not been involved.

Starr, was an imposing figure at six feet seven inches (2 m) tall. His criminal career commenced in 1892 at age sixteen with the robbery of the Nowata Indian Territory (Oklahoma) Depot of $1,700. Starr would lead an amazing life that included bank robbery, the shooting of a U.S. Marshal, deftly maneuvering through the legal system to appeal a death sentence, getting a pardon from President Theodore Roosevelt, becoming a movie star, and then returning to bank robbery.

On March 27, 1915, Starr and seven armed men rode into Stroud with an intent to rob two banks simultaneously. Things did not go as planned. The vault at the Stroud National Bank

was on a time lock, and only $1,600 was in the drawers. According to legend, a child named Lorene Hughes walked into the bank during the robbery, and Starr sat her in a chair and gave her a handful of pennies. If true, the story provides insight into Starr's complex personality.

Paul Curry, a nineteen-year-old man working at his father's grocery store, borrowed a .44-caliber rifle after hearing gunfire at the bank and hid in the alley behind the bank. As Starr approached, Curry fired, striking Starr in the hip.

Starr and several accomplices were arrested, convicted, and sentenced to prison. Starr proved himself a model prisoner and received a pardon after serving but a few years of his twenty-five-year sentence. On February 22, 1921, Starr met his demise during a bank robbery in Harrison, Arkansas.

A Route 66 landmark is the Rock Café. The original owner, Roy Rives, spent three years building the restaurant. To curb construction costs, he resorted to hiring high school students.

It opened for business in August 1939. Even though gas rationing during World War I curtailed travel on Route 66, the café flourished as it also served as a Greyhound bus stop. Indicative of the growth in postwar travel on Route 66, in 1946, the café went to a twenty-four-hour, seven-day-a-week schedule. It was during this period that the attention-grabbing sign, a landmark today, was installed.

The café survived the Route 66 bypass but needed extensive renovation by 1990. Dawn Welch, inspiration for the Sally Carrera character in the animated movie Cars, initiated restoration shortly after acquisition. In 2001, the restaurant was added to the National Register of Historic Places.

A cost share grant from the National Park Service's Route 66 Corridor Preservation Program was awarded in the same year. The owners used the funds to complete a full renovation to original appearance.

In 2008 a fire gutted the structure. It was again restored with funds from the National Park Service Funding and National Trust Southwest Office. It reopened in 2009 and is favorite stop for Route 66 travelers.

EL RENO

The early alignment of Route 66 followed Shepard Avenue, Elm Street, Hoff, Choctaw Avenue, and Wade Street. After 1932, it continued west on Elm to join Rock Island Avenue. Both alignments followed Sunset.

A few miles (5 to 6 km) west of town is Fort Reno. Major General Jesse L. Reno, killed on September 14, 1862, at the Battle of South Mountain during the American Civil War, is the namesake for the fort and community.

The fort was established in the summer of 1874 to protect the Darlington Indian Agency during the Cheyenne uprising. This military post serviced various functions through 1948 with a brief period of closure in 1908. It has been used by the U.S. Department

of Agriculture as a research/experiment station since termination as a military facility.

In 1866, Congress approved legislation allowing Black Americans to enlist in the United States military. Six (later combined into four) all-Black regiments of the Army were created, led by white officers. Dubbed "Buffalo Soldiers" by Native Americans, the 9th and 10th Cavalry were stationed at Fort Reno beginning in 1875 through the early 1880s. One 10th Cavalry soldier and six soldiers of the 9th Cavalry are interred in the Fort Reno Post Cemetery.

In 1908, Fort Reno was designated one of three Army Quartermaster Remount Stations, its primary role through 1948. This included specialized horse breeding and the training of pack mules.

Black Jack, a ceremonial horse used in the funeral processions of Presidents Hoover, Kennedy, and Johnson, as well as General MacArthur, was trained at the fort. This horse was also used in the caisson unit that assisted in the burying of Korean and Vietnam soldiers killed in combat.

During World War II, the base also served as a prisoner of war camp. The incarcerated included German and Italian soldiers captured during the battle of North Africa and Sicily. In 1944, German prisoners built the chapel located north of the parade grounds.

The Fort Reno Post Cemetery is unique. Interred here are soldiers and pioneer citizens from the territorial era as well as Italian and German military personnel in the POW annex.

The fort has a surprisingly lengthy celebrity history. Artist Frederic Remington spent three months at Fort Reno in 1888 producing numerous detailed drawings of cavalry, scouts, Buffalo Soldiers, and the Cheyenne and Arapaho tribes. Aviator Amelia Earhart flew her autogiro at the Fort Reno airstrip in 1931. Will Rogers visited the fort frequently to watch polo matches and horse races.

Postal service at the fort commenced in February of 1877 and culminated with the post office closure in May of 1907. The fort has buildings spanning its entire history, some of which are used for a visitor center and U.S. Cavalry Association Headquarters & Museum.

According to the Oklahoma Historical Society, "El Reno is divided by the 98th Meridian. The eastern side of this dividing line opened to settlement in the Land

CROSSROADS OF AMERICA

El Reno, OK

OKLAHOMA
U S
66

Run of 1889. The western section was included in the April 1892 run that included Cheyenne and Arapaho lands. Additionally, the town was one of two sites selected for land district offices in anticipation of the 1901 land lottery drawings. El Reno was the final selection."

To differentiate the community from another nearby town site, Reno City, and the fort, the post office application approved on June 28, 1889, used the name El Reno. The town is the county seat of Canadian County, Oklahoma, and headquarters for the Cheyenne and Arapaho tribes.

It was at this location the western fork of the Chisholm Trail crossed the North Canadian River. The Chicago, Kansas & Nebraska Railroad, owned by the Chicago, Rock Island & Pacific Railroad after 1891, also forded the river here. El Reno became the crossroads of the main north-south and east-west lines of the transcontinental Chicago, Rock Island & Pacific Railroad. In addition to the railyard, the railroad also constructed division repair shops and a coach-building center. The historic Rock Island Depot, listed on the National Register of Historic Places in 1983, now serves as an anchor for a museum complex operated by the Canadian County Historical Society.

Route 66 broadened the town's dependence on provision of transportation services. A 1936 business directory listed thirty-eight filling stations, twenty-four restaurants, eight tourist camps, and ten hotels.

In recent years, numerous structures associated with Route 66 have been razed. One of the most notable is the Big 8 Motel that opened in the late 1940s and was featured in the movie *Rain Man* starring Dustin Hoffman.

Still, there is a wide array of structures of historical significance from the pre-interstate highway era remaining along various alignments of Route 66. Exemplifying this are the former Avant's Cities Service Station, 220 North Choctaw, and the former Jackson Conoco Service Station, 121 West Wade, built in 1934. These stations are representatives of oil companies' initial endeavors to achieve brand recognition through architecture and design elements.

A tangible link to Route 66 history is Johnnie's Grill located on Rock Island Avenue. Famous for its fried onion burgers, the restaurant opened in 1946. The original building collapsed in 1988, but the current restaurant operates on the same block.

In 1934, the United States Southwestern Reformatory was constructed two miles (3.2 km) west of El Reno. At the time, it was the fifth-largest prison in the United States. The facility was renamed the Federal Reformatory, El Reno in 1938, and then again in the 1970s to the Federal Correctional Institution El Reno.

"I TRAVEL NOT TO GO ANYWHERE BUT TO GO. I TRAVEL FOR TRAVEL'S SAKE. THE GREAT AFFAIR IS TO MOVE."

—ROBERT LOUIS STEVENSON

ELK CITY

In Elk City, the earliest alignment of US 66 followed the Old Postal Road to an intersection with Main Street as it followed 3rd Street through town. This was the route noted in the 1923 *Auto Bluebook*, an early annual guidebook for travelers.

Before the town of Elk City was surveyed and platted in March 1901, along Elk Creek, cattle drives followed the Western Trail through the area heading north to Abilene and Dodge City in Kansas. Two days after completion of the survey, the Choctaw Townsite and Improvement Company began selling town lots. This marked the end of the free-range era in western Oklahoma.

The first post office application filed on March 18, 1901, was under the name Busch. As this resulted in confusion because another western Oklahoma community was named Bush, the application was amended using the name Elk City on July 20, 1907.

After 1910, as the town was located at a junction of the Choctaw, Oklahoma & Gulf Railroad, Wichita Falls & Northwestern Railroad, and Chicago, Rock Island & Pacific Railroad, Elk City developed as a prosperous and vibrant agricultural center. It was also a progressive community. With great fanfare, on October 11, 1915, the Carnegie Library opened. In 1924, the Elk City Junior College was established.

In the summer of 1931, the rural Oklahoma community was the subject of national news coverage. Amid the Dust Bowl and worsening economic crisis, Dr. Michael A. Shadid started a revolutionary initiative to provide area farmers and ranchers with modern medical care. Working with other area doctors, he established the Community Hospital, a cooperative medical facility. For the fee of fifty dollars, one share of stock in the hospital could be purchased. Then, for twenty-five dollars a year, the stockholder would have the benefit of free medical treatment for themselves and their immediate family.

Unlike many rural Oklahoma communities, Elk City had a remarkably diverse economy. By 1911, the city was supporting four banks, four cotton gins, and a cottonseed oil mill. In less than a decade, an ice plant, two broom factories, and two flour mills were also operating in the town. Still, the post–World War I economic recession and then the Great Depression stunted growth for several decades.

Increasingly, the traffic on Route 66 that fueled a growing service industry became an integral component in the town's economy. Indicative of the highway's importance to Elk City, in 1931, the U.S. Highway 66 Association held its annual convention in Elk City. According to most sources, an estimated 20,000 people attended the event that included a parade and rodeo. At this conference, Charles H. Tompkins, former mayor of El Reno, Oklahoma, succeeded Cyrus Avery as president of the association.

In 1948, Reese and Wanda Queenan established their trading post at the junction of US 66 and State Highway 6. During the 1950s, it was a popular attraction with Route 66 travelers.

To differentiate their establishment from other trading posts along the highway, two towering and colorful kachina sculptures were constructed from drums and pipes. The trading post closed in 1980. The kachinas were later refurbished and relocated to the front of the National Route 66 Museum.

Another rare link to Route 66 history is located to the west of town. Built in 1926 for the Route 66 alignment that was used until 1958, the bright-yellow Timber Creek Bridge, a modified Pratt through-truss bridge, is a popular photo op for Route 66 enthusiasts.

Oil companies and wildcatters, freelance oil prospectors, had searched for oil in the area since at least 1910. Then, on November 24, 1947, Shell

STAR COURTS
U.S. HIWAY 66 WEST
ELK CITY, OKLA.

A-366

Oil Company brought in the first producing oil well. Decades later, the Anadarko Basin would become renowned as a leading producer of natural gas and for some of the deepest wells on earth.

Standing in mute testimony to the oil industry in Elk City is Parker Drilling Rig #114 that was originally built in the 1960s to drill shafts for underground nuclear testing. At 181 feet (55.2 m), nearly seventeen stories, this is one of the world's tallest oil rigs.

The Anadarko Basin Museum of Natural History, closed as of this writing, is in the old Casa Grande Hotel. This was the host hotel for the U.S. Highway 66 Association National Convention on April 27, 1931. Listed on the National Register of Historic Places in 1995, the hotel was built in 1928.

The Elk City Museum Complex, which includes the National Route 66 Museum, a Farm and Ranch Museum, the National Transportation Museum, the Blacksmith Museum, and the Beutler Brothers Rodeo Hall, an expansive rodeo exhibit, is a popular destination for Route 66 enthusiasts. The rich, diverse, and colorful history of Elk City including its association with Route 66 is chronicled in the complex.

CHAPTER FIVE

TEXAS

LONE STAR STATE

MCLEAN

In 1984, diminutive McLean had the dubious distinction of being the last town on Route 66 in the Texas Panhandle to be bypassed by I-40. In an instant, the never-ending stream of traffic that flowed through town on 1st Street and Railroad Street slowed to a trickle. This had a devastating effect on the town's economy, and it has never recovered.

As of 2019, the population of McLean was 939 people. This is a dramatic decline from 1940 when the population was more than 1,500 people.

Interestingly, the town has a direct connection with the sinking of the Titanic. That story is told through artifacts on display at the Devil's Rope Museum, a museum dedicated to the history of barbed wire, that is housed in a former brassiere factory. This factory led to McLean proudly proclaiming itself "The Uplift Capital of the World" on a billboard entering town. This building also houses the Texas Route 66 Museum, which showcases over 700 items from along the Texas Route 66 stretch.

Alfred Rowe was a brilliant entrepreneur with a colorful background. He was born to British parents in Peru and was educated in England. After extensive agricultural studies, he traveled to Texas with plans of establishing a ranch.

To learn the trade from the ground up, he worked as a cowboy for the legendary Charles Goodnight. After acquiring vast land holdings, he established the 200,000-acre (80,937 ha) RO Ranch, the largest in the Texas Panhandle, in partnership with his brothers, Vincent and Bernard.

After the Choctaw, Oklahoma & Texas Railroad established a switchyard and section house with a well, Rowe donated adjoining lands that were officially platted as a town site on December 3, 1902. The town was named in honorarium of William Pinkney McLean, a hero of the War of Texas Independence and the state's first railroad commissioner.

In 1901, Rowe married Constance Ethel Kingsley, a cousin of the British author Charles Kingsley. In 1910, he moved his family to England and left Jack Hall to manage the ranch and keep its records. Rowe often returned twice a year to visit the ranch and take care of related business.

In April 1912, Rowe booked passage on the maiden voyage of the Titanic. His body was recovered by the Cable Ship Mackay-Bennett, transported back to England, and interred in Liverpool. The Rowe family ran the RO Ranch until 1917, when it was sold to W. J. Lewis.

Rowe and Kingsley streets in McLean are tangible links to the family's association with the town. The old Rowe Cemetery, located to the south of McLean in the former town of Rowe, is another link to their association with the Panhandle.

By 1910, McLean was a thriving community. The business district included three general mercantile stores, a bank, a newspaper, and several blacksmith shops with livery stables. The economy was diversified with petroleum-related businesses and a service industry that met the needs of travelers on the Ozark Trails Highway that connected St. Louis, Missouri, with Las Vegas,

New Mexico. This segment of the economy boomed after certification of Route 66 in 1926.

In 1929, Phillips Petroleum opened one of the company's first stations in Texas in McLean. The cottage-style station remained in operation until 1977. Renovation of the station's exterior to its original appearance makes it a favored photo stop for Route 66 travelers.

In September 1942, construction of the McLean Permanent Alien Internment Camp east of town commenced. This POW camp for German troops captured during battles in North Africa remained operational through July 1, 1945.

The traffic on Route 66 enabled the town's economy to be resilient.

It survived the drought of the Dust Bowl, the Great Depression, and the resultant collapse of agricultural prices. It also was able to endure the growth of surrounding towns, nearby Pampa becoming the county's industrial center, and the decline of the oil industry. It was the bypass of Route 66 that severed McLean from its last economic lifeline, and this proved to be a harsh blow from which the city has yet to recover.

In 2004, a large section of the central business district with brick-lined streets was listed on the National Register of Historic Places. This did not curb the decline or the loss of historic buildings such as the Hindman Hotel and Avalon Theater.

The Route 66 renaissance has had a positive effect on McLean. The Red River Steakhouse, a relatively recent addition to the community, consistently garners favorable reviews from travelers for its food as well as ambiance. Nearby is the circa 1956 Cactus Inn Motel that was purchased by Angela Moreland in 2020. An extensive renovation has given the historic property a new lease on life.

AMARILLO

Route 66 followed various courses through Amarillo as the highway and the city evolved. It originally followed 6th Avenue through the historic San Jacinto district. The highway also used Amarillo Boulevard, Triangle Drive, Fillmore Street, SW 9th Avenue, and NE 8th Avenue.

For New Mexico traders in the early to mid-nineteenth century, the large muddy playa known as Amarillo or Wild Horse Lake was a vital oasis on the notoriously dry high plains. The playa was equally important to the Fort Worth & Denver Railroad that began surveying a rail line across the Panhandle in 1886.

A group of Colorado City merchants chose the site to establish stores as a supply center after learning of plans to build a railroad siding near the Playa. J. T. Berry platted a townsite named Oneida after his arrival from Abilene.

Berry and store owners conspired to make the new town, now called Amarillo, the Potter county seat. According to local legend, as most of the counties' registered voters were LX Ranch employees, a questionable arrangement was made with the ranch's owner. In exchange for votes, if the new town were selected as the county seat, a voter would be deeded a lot.

With completion of the railroad to Amarillo in October 1887, Amarillo boomed as a cattle-marketing and supply center. After the passenger station and freight depot were built near the tracks, people from the surrounding area began moving to Amarillo. Prospective land buyers were brought in by chartered excursion trains.

By 1890, Amarillo had emerged as one of the world's busiest cattle-shipping points in the country. With the addition of rail lines and a switchyard by the Kansas City Southern Railroad, Pecos & Northern Texas Railroad, and the Chicago, Rock Island & Gulf Railroad in 1903, and additional stock yards, the town grew to be the largest community in the Texas Panhandle.

In 1902, St. Anthony's Hospital, the first hospital in the Panhandle, was built. In the same year, the Amarillo Light and Water Company was established. This marked the commencement of Amarillo's transformation from a western frontier town into a modern, progressive community.

In 1913, an Arkansas tourism entrepreneur, William "Coin" Harvey, launched the Ozark Trail Association. The goal was to develop and promote an improved highway for automobiles that connected St. Louis, Missouri, and Las Vegas, New Mexico. Development of the road system would become a pivotal moment in Amarillo history.

In June 1917, the Ozark Trail Association held their convention in Amarillo. The focus was development of the trail system in the Panhandle and eastern New Mexico. Portions of the trail system were used as the course for US 66 in 1926.

The original alignment of Route 66 bisects the U.S. Route 66-Sixth Street Historic District, thirteen blocks of the San Jacinto Heights Addition west of Amarillo's central business district. The district was added to the National Register of Historic Places in 1994.

This area was initially developed as a suburb that was linked by a streetcar line. Preserved in the area are a diverse array of buildings representing various architectural styles including Spanish Revival, Art Deco, and Art Moderne.

The GoldenLight Cafe opened at 209 West 6th Avenue in 1946. It is the oldest continuously operated café on Route 66 in Amarillo and is internationally known for its grilled green chili cheeseburgers.

The Natatorium, known locally as "the Nat," is located at 2705 West 6th Ave. It was originally built in 1922 to encircle an outdoor public swimming pool and then was converted into an enclosure. It was transformed into a ballroom in 1926. For decades, it was a focal point of the city's entertainment district. Tommy Dorsey and Duke Ellington are but two of the major acts to play at "the Nat."

On June 23, 1949, Amarillo made national headlines with a sensationalized crime, scandal, and trial that involved a celebrity, sex, and a manhunt along Route 66 in three states. Amarillo resident W. A. "Tex" Thornton was an oil-field firefighter with a legendary reputation.

He checked into the Park Plaza Motel, cabin number 18, at 612 Northeast 8th Street, Route 66. Shortly after 9:00 a.m. the following morning, Jessie Mae Walker, the motel maid, discovered Thornton's nude body in the rear bedroom of the cabin.

An intense manhunt was launched along Route 66 from Tucumcari, New Mexico, to Oklahoma City, Oklahoma. Months later, the suspects were arrested, one in Washington, D.C., and one in Michigan. The trial that commenced on May 7, 1950, garnered national headlines for days.

A Route 66 landmark is the Big Texan Steak Ranch. It was originally established in March 1960 by R. J. "Bob" Lee on Route 66. With an ambiance that mimicked a western movie set, a horseback mounted cowboy that greeted guests, and a towering 60-foot (18.3 m) neon lit cowboy sign, the restaurant was an instant hit with travelers.

In November 1960, Lee launched an innovative promotional campaign that continues to be a major attraction. The one-hour Steak Challenge was a 72-ounce (2 kg) steak, baked potato, salad, shrimp cocktail, and a bread roll with butter. Anyone that can consume the dinner in one hour gets it for free. Today, the challenge is broadcast as a live feed on their website.

In September 1969, a new restaurant was built along I-40 that was being built to bypass Route 66. Most of the complex was destroyed in a July 1976 fire. In January 1978, the current Big Texan restaurant opened, and a Texas themed motel and Texas-shaped swimming pool were added to the complex in 1983.

GLENRIO

Route 66 coursed through the center of Glenrio on its one primary street. The postwar growth of traffic that escalated in the 1950s resulted in this street being transformed into a four-lane corridor. This segment of highway was added to the National Register of Historic Places in 2007.

Glenrio is in Deaf Smith County, named for Erastus "Deaf" Smith, a famous scout of the Texas Revolution. This is a border town that has at various times appeared on maps as Glenrio, New Mexico, and Glenrio, Texas. Further confusing the situation was the initial establishment of a post office on the New Mexico side of the community. But the depot where the mail arrived was on the Texas side.

Even into the Route 66 era the town remained uniquely divided. Deaf Smith County was dry, so bars and businesses that sold liquor were located on the New Mexico side of town. But as gasoline taxes were higher in New Mexico, service stations and garages opened on the Texas side.

The origins of this community date to the surveying and division of the surrounding area into farms in 1905.

The following year, the Chicago, Rock Island & Gulf Railway established a station and siding at Glenrio. With construction of feed lots, the community thrived as a shipping point for an array of agricultural products and as a supply center.

With establishment of the Ozark Trails Highway, a precursor to US 66 in the Panhandle, the town's economic base expanded. By 1920, the business district in Glenrio included a hardware store, land office, cafés, garages, general store, and a newspaper office. The *Glenrio Tribune* was published from 1910 to 1934.

The town's proximity to the state line led the state of Texas to build a "welcome center" here in the late 1930s. An article in *The Amarillo Daily News*, November 15, 1946, about this welcome center provides a snapshot of the inception of the travel boom that began in the postwar era. "The State Highway Department's information bureau located at the Texas–New Mexico line on US 66 at Glenrio furnished 288 cars with maps of Texas and places of interest. Among the cars stopping for information were 65 from California, 25 from Illinois, 11 from Indiana, 24 from Michigan, and 13 from Missouri. Three cars from Canada and one from the Canal Zone also stopped for information." The facility appears briefly in the film adaptation of *The Grapes of Wrath* released in 1940.

Drought and the Great Depression decimated agriculture in the area. Then, in 1955, the town was dealt another severe blow when the depot was closed. Suspension of service and the removal of rails followed a short time later.

The long-shuttered Texas Longhorn Motel and Café once promoted with a sign that read "First Stop in Texas" on one side and "Last Stop in Texas" on the other is a popular photo op for Route 66 travelers. These structures date to about 1950.

Before establishing this facility, Homer and Margaret Ehresman opened the State Line Bar on the New Mexico side of the state line in 1934. Margaret ran the post office from this location. For a brief time, they also operated a business in Endee west of Glenrio.

By the summer of 1973, as construction of I-40 one mile (1.6 km) to the north neared completion, most businesses in Glenrio had closed. One of the last businesses was the State Line Bar that had been purchased by Albert and Dessie Leach in the late 1950s. This bar was the scene of a brutal murder on July 10, 1973.

Dessie opened the bar and was alone when a couple from Amarillo heading west in a motorhome became her

first customers that afternoon. The second customer was John Wayne Lee, a friendly young man that ordered a beer and asked the other customers if they would play pool.

Shortly after the Amarillo couple continued their westward journey, Cornelia Tapia, who lived in an apartment behind the bar, saw Dessie Leach stagger out of the back door of the bar. Her dress was soaked in blood. She had been stabbed four times and died before she could be transported to the hospital in Tucumcari, New Mexico. Lee fled east on Route 66 and was apprehended without a struggle a few hours later in Vega, Texas.

The State Line Bar closed after the murder and it never reopened. Dessie's husband Albert moved to nearby San Jon, New Mexico, where he raised horses.

Most remaining structures in Glenrio are from the period 1930 to 1960. These include the Texas Longhorn Café and Motel, the Little Juarez Diner built in a manner to imitate the popular Valentine Diners, and the adobe constructed service station at the west end of town. All seventeen of the buildings that constitute the business district are listed in the National Register of Historic Places.

At the state line on the west end of town, two distinct alignments of Route 66 are present. The post-1955 alignment sweeps north toward Bard where it is truncated by I-40. The earliest alignment continues southwest toward San Jon through the ghost town of Endee.

Glenrio is also considered a ghost town as the population is less than five people. Its picturesque, abandoned buildings and ruins that illustrate the devastation wrought in communities resultant of the bypass of US 66 make it a favored stop for Route 66 travelers.

> "I HAVE FOUND OUT THAT THERE AIN'T NO SURER WAY TO FIND OUT WHETHER YOU LIKE PEOPLE OR HATE THEM THAN TO TRAVEL WITH THEM."
>
> —MARK TWAIN

CHAPTER SIX

NEW MEXICO

LAND OF ENCHANTMENT

TUCUMCARI

Route 66 followed Tucumcari Boulevard through Tucumcari. This fueled the creation of a new and thriving business district corridor and the decline of the city's historic center that had initially developed along the railroad. Today, the international interest in Route 66 is fostering a renaissance along that highway corridor in Tucumcari.

The town itself dates to the 1901 establishment of a railroad siding on the Chicago, Rock Island & Pacific Railroad. But the town site and surrounding area is steeped in myth, legend, and historic references dating to 1777.

Dominating the southern horizon is 4,951-foot (1.5 km) Tucumcari Mountain. Local legend has it that the mountain is named for two love-struck Native Americans: Tocom and Kari. But Oklahoman linguist Elliot Canoga has a more grounded explanation. According to Canoga, *tukamukaru* is a Comanche word that references lying in wait for an approach.

As romantic as legends are, another explanation for the name is the discovery of a burial record from a Spanish expedition dated 1777 that notes the capture of a Comanche woman and her child in a battle at

Cuchuncari, which is located near this mountain. It is thought that the word Cuchuncari could be the initial form of the name Tuchumcari.

On the dry, high desert plain, Lake Tucumcari was a true oasis. So, it is not surprising to learn that for centuries trade routes crossed in the area. In the modern era, one of the most famous of these was the Goodnight-Loving Trail, popular for cattlemen driving herds from Texas to the railroads in Denver or to northern prairies in Wyoming.

The tent city established at the site of Tucumcari as a railroad construction camp was referenced as Six Shooter Siding. For reasons unknown, the first post office application was filed using the name Douglas. But in 1902, the application for a post office was amended and the town became Tucumcari.

The railroad was the cornerstone of the town's initial economy. In 1901, a junction was completed between the Southern Pacific Railroad and the Chicago, Rock Island & Pacific. As early as 1905, four passenger trains, two mail trains, and two freight trains made daily stops in Tucumcari.

A modern, Spanish Mission–styled railroad depot was built in 1926 by the Chicago, Rock Island & Pacific

Railroad for joint use with the Southern Pacific Railroad's Golden State Limited. The last passenger train to use the depot was in 1968. The renovated facility now houses the Tucumcari Railroad Museum.

As the city was in a rich agricultural area, ranching and farming enabled development of a well-diversified economy in the years bracketing World War I. This was enhanced with development of a service industry to meet the need of travelers on the Ozark Trails highway network connecting Saint Louis, Missouri, El Paso, Texas, and Las Vegas, New Mexico. Sections of this highway would later be designated US 66. And the establishment of US 54 that continues to serve as a major trucking route further strengthened the service industry sector.

"I TAKE TO THE OPEN ROAD, HEALTHY, FREE, THE WORLD BEFORE ME."

—WALT WHITMAN

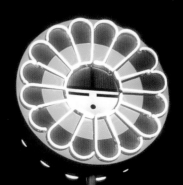
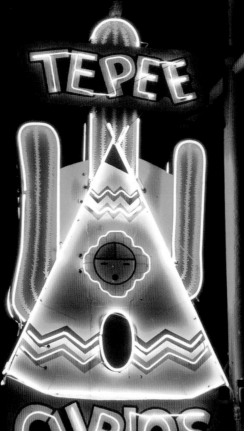

The droughts of the late 1920s and early 1930s curtailed farming. The bypass of Route 66 in 1985 was another crippling blow. The population has been in decline for decades, from 8,419 people in 1950 to 5,050 people counted in a recent census.

Still, Tucumcari exemplifies why Route 66 is often referenced as a string of time capsules. The highway corridor through town is amply peppered with an array of sites that are tangible links to Route 66 history.

The renovated Motel Safari, with its historic "Clyde the Camel" neon sign, dates to 1960. One of the most photographed properties on Route 66 is the Blue Swallow Motel that opened in 1939.

The Roadrunner Lodge aptly illustrates post–World War II Route 66 motel history. Though it is difficult to discern today, there are two motels in this complex. The older portion, on the west side of the complex, was built in 1947 as La Plaza Court. In the early 1950s, the motel was renovated and expanded by converting the individual attached garages into rooms.

Agnes Leatherwood opened Leatherwood Manor on the east side in 1964. It was a modern two-story motel that mimicked those offered by the chains such as Travel Lodge or Rodeway Inn. Several years later, after acquisition of the La Plaza Court, the two motels were renovated as a single property.

The remodel included extension of the roofline of the Leatherwood lobby to cover both properties. A multi-room suite was created by combining the lobby and manager's rooms of the La Plaza Court. In early 2014, after years of closure, the motel was acquired by David Brenner and renovated to its appearance in the mid-1960s.

Tucumcari is also a progressive community with an eye on the future. The exhibits at the Mesalands Community College's Dinosaur Museum and Natural Science Laboratory are on par with displays at museums such as the Smithsonian Institution. This community college has also pioneered development of the Wind Energy Technology Program at the North American Wind Research and Training Center in Tucumcari.

SANTA FE

Before the loop from Santa Rosa to Albuquerque was bypassed in 1937, Route 66 followed a confusing array of streets through the historic heart of Santa Fe. This included Cerrillos Road, De Vargas, Don Gaspar, Old Santa Fe Trail, San Francisco, Alameda, Water, Lincoln, Washington, and Grant.

Archeologists have determined that Pueblo villages occupied the site of Santa Fe in about 1050 CE. Studies estimate that they were abandoned at least two centuries before the arrival of Spanish explorers.

A small farming community was established at the site in 1607 by Spanish immigrants. Don Juan de Oñate, the first Governor-General of New Mexico, established the territorial capital in 1598 at San Juan Pueblo located about twenty-five miles (40.2 km) north of Santa Fe. Don Pedro de Peralta, appointed Governor-General in 1609, moved the capital to present day Santa Fe the following year.

On order of the Spanish Crown, the Palace of the Governors was built in 1610. This is the oldest public building in continuous use in the continental United States. It was one of the few buildings in Santa Fe to survive the Pueblo Revolt in 1680 when the Pueblo nation revolted against the Spanish colonists in New Mexico and drove them south.

Santa Fe was sacked and most of the buildings were burned. The city was reclaimed in 1692 when Don Diego de Vargas reconquered the region.

When Mexico gained its independence from Spain, Santa Fe was designated the capital of the New Mexico province. Shortly afterward, in September 1821, William Becknell opened the Santa Fe Trail from Franklin, Missouri, and the city became a prosperous trade center.

2305-30

On August 18, 1846, General Stephen Watts Kearny took Santa Fe and raised the American flag over the Plaza. The Treaty of Guadalupe Hidalgo, ceding New Mexico and California to the United States, was signed two years later. In March 1863, the Confederate flag of General Henry Hastings Sibley flew over Santa Fe until his defeat.

The ancient city was brought into the modern era when it was connected to the east and west coast by telegraph in 1868. Transition escalated when the Atchison, Topeka & Santa Fe Railway reached Santa Fe in 1880.

Extensive lawlessness in the New Mexico territory led President Rutherford B. Hayes to appoint Lew Wallace as territorial governor. Wallace was also an author, and he wrote most of the manuscript for the book *Ben-Hur* at the Palace of the Governors.

When New Mexico gained statehood in 1912, many people were drawn to Santa Fe's dry climate as a cure for tuberculosis. Meanwhile, the city continued to evolve as the region's cultural center during this period. The Museum of New Mexico opened in 1909. In 1917, the Museum of Fine Arts, now called the New Mexico Museum of Art, was built. This blending of cultures in an ancient setting fueled Santa Fe's image as an "exotic" city.

Establishment of the National Old Trails Road opened the city to a flood of tourists. Edsel Ford noted in his travel journal dated July 6, 1915, that Santa Fe was, "very interesting."

In her best-selling book *By Motor to The Golden Gate* published in 1916, Emily Post devoted a chapter to this city and painted vivid word pictures about its colorful, vibrant, and singular nature.

In 1926, the Old Santa Fe Association was established "to preserve and maintain the ancient landmarks, historical structures and traditions of Old Santa Fe, to guide its growth and development in such a way as to sacrifice as little as possible of that unique charm born of age, tradition and environment, which are the priceless assets and heritage of Old Santa Fe." This was also the year that US 66 was certified.

Route 66 was realigned in 1937, and Santa Fe was bypassed. A tangible link to the city's association with that highway is the El Rey Court.

Built at 1862 Cerillos Road, Route 66, the El Rey Inn opened in 1936. It was designed in a style that blended Spanish Colonial and Pueblo architectural styles by the company that built the El Vado Motel in Albuquerque.

Historical integrity of the property and its design was maintained through the addition of rooms, upgrades, and even incorporation of the neighboring Alamo Court into the complex. This has contributed to the motel's popularity with Route 66 enthusiasts. A unique aspect of the Ely Rey Court is that their five acres (2 ha) of landscaped gardens double as a nationally recognized bird sanctuary.

The time capsule feel of the neighborhood is enhanced by The Pantry restaurant that describes itself as "Santa Fe's meeting and eating place since 1948."

La Fonda on The Plaza exemplifies the unique nature of Santa Fe. Records indicate that this hotel sits on the site of the town's first inn built in about 1608. This is the oldest continuously occupied hotel property in the United States.

The current hotel was built in 1922. It was designed by architects Mary Elizabeth Jane Colter and John Gaw Meem to mimic buildings built during the Spanish Colonial period. There was extensive use of hand carved beams, stained glass skylights, and a 25-foot (7.6 m) cathedral ceiling.

In 1925, the hotel was acquired by the Atchison, Topeka & Santa Fe Railway and then leased to the Fred Harvey Company. It remained a "Harvey House" until 1968. It is still a premier hotel in the city and is a member of Historic Hotels of America, a program founded in 1989 by The National Trust for Historic Preservation.

GRANTS

Route 66 follows Santa Fe Avenue through Grants. The four lane corridor hints at the level of traffic that flowed through town before US 66 was bypassed by I-40.

Shortly before the Civil War, Don Diego Antonio Chavez established a homestead and ranch on the south side of the Rio San Jose near the present site of Grants. Don Jesus Blea acquired the ranch and expanded the land holdings in 1872. He named it Los Alamitos.

John, Lewis, and Angus Grant, railroad contractors with the Atlantic & Pacific Railroad, predecessor to the Atchison, Topeka & Santa Fe Railway, established a construction camp at this site in 1881. With completion of the railroad to this point and the addition of a depot, siding, and water and coaling station, the camp was designated Grants Station.

A small village grew around the camp. The initial post office application was filed in 1882 under the name Grant. In 1935 it was amended, for reasons unknown, to Grants. This is the county seat of Cibola County.

The town grew slowly and steadily with an economy built on the railroad serving as a vital supply center for the area. Logging in the nearby Zuni Mountains and agriculture were also important to the development of Grants. During the Great Depression logging declined. With the creation of Bluewater Reservoir, agriculture became a major component of the area's economy. Grants was even promoted for a brief time as the "Carrot Capital" of the United States.

After 1916, as traffic on the National Old Trails Road began to increase exponentially, a corresponding modern service industry developed. Still, Grants remained an isolated rural community. The town was not fully electrified until 1929.

That was the year that Grants garnered national headlines for its association with several aeronautical milestones. Transcontinental Air Transport, a pioneering passenger airline that would evolve into TWA, established a terminal in the city. At the Western New Mexico Aviation Heritage Museum at the Grants-Milan Airport, a restored 51-foot (15.5 m) TAT beacon tower and power shed and large concrete directional arrow is preserved.

On the morning of Tuesday September 3, 1929, a TAT plane named the City of San Francisco departed Albuquerque's airfield bound for Los Angeles, California. On board were five passengers, two pilots, and a courier. Resultant of stormy weather, about 45 minutes after takeoff, the pilot diverted from course and crashed into the mountainous terrain of Mt. Taylor near Grants, New Mexico. This was one of the first commercial passenger airline disasters.

In 1958, another air disaster put Grants on the front page of newspapers throughout the world.

AAA directories chronicle the evolution of the city's service industry resultant of Route 66. The *Hotel, Garage & Service Station Directory* published in 1927 has but one entry for Grants, the St. Morris Garage. In Jack Rittenhouse's *A Guide Book to Highway 66*, his detailed summary of Grants notes two hotels, five motels, numerous cafés, stores, and repair facilities. The 1954 edition of the AAA *Western Accommodations Directory* lists numerous motels, garages, and cafés.

Preserved at the expansive New Mexico Mining Museum with the world's only simulated underground uranium mine are relics from the

"Dateline March 3, Grants, N. M. (AP) – Famed producer Mike Todd perished in flames early Saturday with three others in the crash of his twin-engine airplane "The Lucky Liz," named for his actress wife Elizabeth Taylor. The executive-type plane plunged with tremendous force, exploded and burned in the Zuni Mountains of western New Mexico southwest of Grants at 2:05 a.m. in a storm."

city's mining history. Unlike many southwestern communities, mining was not a large contributor to the town's economy until 1950. That was the year that Navajo shepherd Paddy Martinez discovered a rich uranium-bearing outcrop at the foot of Haystack Mountain.

Surveys noted that in 1958, New Mexico was the second-largest uranium ore producer in the United States. All this mining activity was concentrated in area known as the Grants Mineral Belt. Active mining continued until 1998.

The mining industry, and Route 66, fueled an era of prosperity in Grants. And both are still impacting the city.

The Environmental Protection Agency is currently dealing with the toxic legacy of uranium mining. Families in Grant paid a high price for the prosperity as those involved with uranium mining have been afflicted with a disproportionate number of cancer cases.

The bypass of Route 66 had a devastating effect on the local economy. But today, the renewed interest in Route 66 has provided restaurants and motels with a financial boost.

The Sands Motel is a tangible link to Route 66 history. It dates to about 1950. Supposedly, Elvis Presley stayed in room 123 on several tours.

Grants is the gateway to numerous national parks, monuments, and Native American pueblos. This includes Chaco Canyon, El Malpais, El Morro, Laguna, and the Acoma pueblo also known as "Sky City" that is considered the oldest continuously inhabited community in the United States.

GALLUP

Route 66 followed several different courses through town. The earliest alignment turned onto 1st Street and then followed Coal Street. This is one block off the four-lane alignment of Route 66 used for more than forty years.

A Westward Overland Stagecoach stop was established at this site in 1880. An Atlantic & Pacific Railroad construction camp, saloons, and general store were added in 1881.

The namesake for the community is David L. Gallup. He was an auditor and paymaster for the Atlantic & Pacific Railroad. He later served as the company's comptroller in the New York City headquarters.

From its inception, the town was an important supply center for travelers, for ranchers, and for the Navajo families that lived in the area. It was also a primary shipping point for cattle, wool, hides, and forest products. As it was in a rural area, in the first decades of the twentieth century, Gallup became an important stop for travelers on the National Old Trails Road and then Route 66.

Discovery of rich deposits of coal in the area during the 1870s transformed the village. In 1895, the western New Mexico railroad divisional terminal was established in Gallup. The terminal included repair and maintenance shops, a depot, and a hotel referenced by Emily Post.

In *By Motor to the Golden Gate* published in 1916, Post noted, "After leaving Acoma, you drive again long and tediously but without serious hindrance to Gallup. At Gallup there is a hotel, a small frame, frontier type of building. But by the time we reached it we agreed that it would be more of an experience to spend the night under the stars. How much the beauty of the stars would have tempted us had the hotel been more inviting I am not very sure."

Indicative of the Gallup's importance as a divisional terminal, in 1918, a modern two-story station was built in the Mission Revival style. Designed by renowned architect Mary Elizabeth Jane Colter, the El Navajo Hotel attached to the depot was opened by the Fred Harvey Company in 1923.

Resultant of the post–World War II decline in passenger rail travel, the hotel was closed in the early 1950s. To accommodate widening of Route 66, it was demolished in 1957.

With the railroad consolidating operations, divisional terminals were consolidated. This led to the closing of the Santa Fe Railway Depot. It later reopened as an unstaffed Amtrak station. Shortly after the city's acquisition of the building, it was renovated in 1996.

It now houses Angela's Café as well as the Gallup Cultural Center operated by the Southwest Indian Foundation. In addition to an Amtrack passenger waiting area, the Gallup Visitor Center relocated to the station in 2004.

The Gallup Cultural Center houses a Storyteller Museum and Gallery of the Masters showcasing Native American arts and culture. There are also exhibits on weaving, sandpainting, silversmithing, the railroad, and historic Route 66. The gift shop features handicrafts created by local Acoma, Zuni, Navajo, Hopi, and other Native American artisans.

At the Gallup Cultural Center a statue of Navajo Chief Manuelito created by sculptor Tim Washburn stands in the plaza. Next to the plaza a 12-foot (3.7 m) bronze statue honors the World War II military Navajo Code Talkers by famous Navajo/Ute sculptor Oreland Joe.

Richardson Trading Company is another manifestation of the city's rich Native American heritage. Dating to 1913, this is a true trading post unlike the classic tourist traps along Route 66. Authentic Native American rugs, jewelry, and other handicrafts are available for sale. But the store's principal clients are Native Americans that pawn or trade goods during winter months and reclaim them in the spring.

A landmark for Route 66 enthusiasts as well as fans of Hollywood history is the El Rancho Hotel. Joe Massaglia constructed the El Rancho Hotel in 1936 along US 66 for R. E. Griffith, brother of the famous movie director D. W. Griffith. It was designed to mimic a large, rambling rustic ranch house.

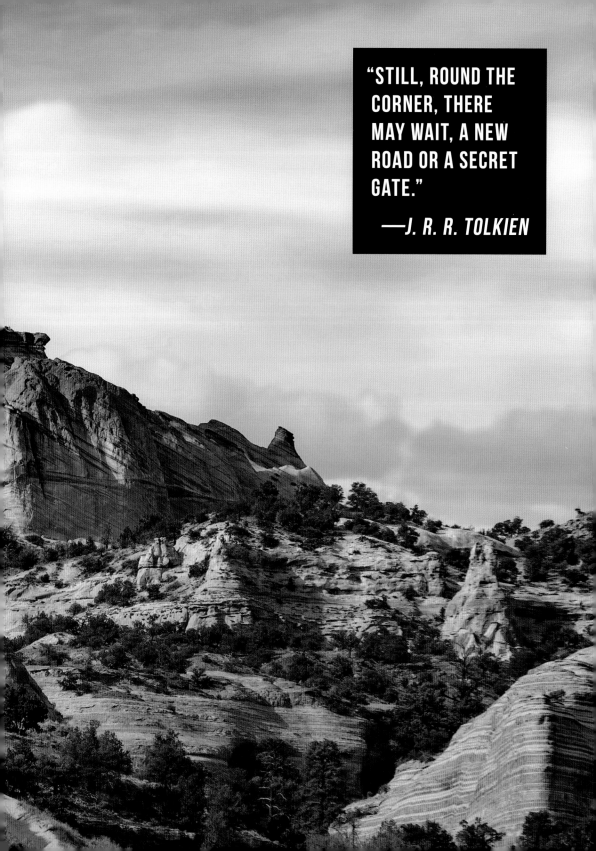

"STILL, ROUND THE CORNER, THERE MAY WAIT, A NEW ROAD OR A SECRET GATE."

—*J. R. R. TOLKIEN*

Griffith had toured in the area a few years prior. The stunning landscapes in the area had led him to encourage his brother to consider filming on location in western New Mexico.

The El Rancho Hotel became a focal point for film crews. It also became a resort haven for celebrities, and as a result, was popular with Route 66 travelers. It continued to be linked to Hollywood and the movie industry until the mid-1960s.

The lobby mezzanine is adorned with autographed framed photos of celebrities that have stayed at the hotel. The list of celebrities includes Harpo Mark, Humphrey Bogart, John Wayne, Kirk Douglas, Ronald Reagan, Spencer Tracy, Errol Flynn, Gary Cooper, and Gregory Peck.

By the mid-1960s, the hotel had faded from prominence. Its continued decline resulted in closure in 1987 and consideration of demolition by the city. Armand Ortega, owner of several area trading posts, bought the hotel and initiated renovation. It now provides guests with an opportunity to experience the charm of a resort hotel of the mid-1950s.

There is an array of tangible links to the Route 66 era in Gallup including original signage on motels, garages, and cafés. A notable landmark is Earl's Family Restaurant at 1400 East Highway 66 that originally opened in 1947 as Earl's Park 'N' Eat. Native American artists sell their wares on the portico as they have since the 1950s.

CHAPTER SEVEN

ARIZONA

GRAND CANYON STATE

HOLBROOK

Route 66 followed Navajo Boulevard and Hopi Drive through Holbrook. This resulted in a shift of the historic business district that had developed along the railroad, Bucket of Blood Street, and SW Central Avenue.

Initial settlement in the area was at Horsehead Crossing near the junction of the Rio Puerco and Little Colorado River several miles (11 km) to the southwest of present-day Holbrook. John Young, son of Mormon pioneer Brigham Young, established a camp for the cutting of railroad ties at that site in 1881.

The Atlantic & Pacific Railroad established a construction camp and then a siding at the site of Holbrook shortly afterward. It was named for H.R. Holbrook, a railroad engineer.

Establishment of the railroad was the cornerstone for the development of expansive ranching and sheep herding enterprises in the area. Until it was broken up in 1902, the Aztec Land & Cattle Company controlled more than one million acres (404,686 ha). This was the largest ranch in the Arizona territory and the second largest ranch in the United States.

The town of Holbrook quickly developed a reputation for lawlessness and violence. Two legendary frontier era lawmen were associated with Holbrook.

Burton C. Mossman was a cowboy employed by the Aztec Land & Cattle Company. By the age of twenty he was working as the ranch foreman and within a few years had developed a reputation for bringing cattle rustlers to justice.

Mossman and a partner operated a stage line in addition to ranching. He was elected sheriff of Navajo County in 1898. Holbrook was the county seat.

In 1901, Oakes Murphy, territorial governor, authorized the re-establishment of the Arizona Rangers and appointed Mossman to be the first captain. This illustrates the reputation Mossman had earned while working as sheriff.

A shootout in Holbrook made Apache County Sheriff Commodore Perry Owens a legend in the annals of history. In September 1887, Owens arrived in Holbrook to serve an arrest warrant on Andy Blevins for horse theft. Blevins and his family had built a rustling empire in

the Mogollon Rim Country. They had also played a bloody role in the Pleasant Valley War.

According to reports by witnesses, John Blevins, Andy's brother, was at the stable when the sheriff arrived on that day in September 1887 and ran to warn Andy. The ensuing gun battle lasted less than five minutes. Andy was mortally wounded. Mose Roberts, a family friend, and fifteen-year-old brother Sam Houston Blevins were dead. John had been shot through the shoulder. Owens was uninjured.

The Blevins House, a private residence with a monument at the street commemorating the gunfight, still stands on Joy Nevin Avenue. It is but one of several landmarks from the territorial era in Holbrook.

The railroad depot built of locally quarried stone dates to 1882. Across the street is the infamous Bucket of Blood Saloon that dates to 1886. It was originally called Terrell's Cottage Saloon but was renamed after an epic gunfight that left what looked like "buckets of blood" on the saloon floor.

The Navajo County Courthouse, now a museum, was built in 1898. The jail was shipped as a whole unit from Kansas City and was set in the basement during construction. The courthouse, more specifically the courthouse jail, figures prominently in the story of a morbidly comedic incident that occurred in 1899.

A territorial statute required sheriffs to issue invitations whenever an execution was scheduled. Navajo County Sheriff F. J. Wattron complied by having professional invitations printed. They were sent to leaders in the community as well as select business owners. The gilt-edged cards read, "You are hereby cordially invited to attend the hanging of one GEORGE SMILEY, Murderer. His soul will be swung into eternity on Dec. 8, 1899, at 2 o'clock p.m., sharp. Latest methods in the art of scientific strangulation will be employed and everything possible will be done to make the surroundings cheerful and the execution a success."

The invitation was brought to the attention of President William McKinley. He immediately chastised the territorial governor and a 30 day stay of execution was ordered. Smiley was executed on January 8, 1900.

The long-closed Higgins House is a landmark of note. It has an association with territorial history, the national Old Trails Road, Route 66, and World War II.

Purportedly the oldest building in Holbrook, it was built in 1881 or 1882 by Pedro Montaño. Additions were made in 1883. In 1884 James and Maggie Higgins acquired the property and established a boarding house. With further expansion, it became the Brunswick Hotel in 1889. An upper floor was used as a dance hall and Masonic lodge.

For a brief period in the 1930s, the west wing of the Brunswick Hotel was used as Holbrook's hospital. With further additions, it became the Arizona Hotel. Then, in the 1940s, it was expanded and named Arizona Rancho, a hotel/motel complex. Leased by Fullerton Junior College during World War II, the hotel housed pilot candidates training at nearby Park Field for U.S.

Navy service. Even though it was several blocks from Route 66, the hotel prospered through the 1950s.

Tourism has been an important part of Holbrook's economy since at least the era of the National Old Trails Road. The city remains the gateway to the Painted Desert and the Petrified Forest National Park, the only national park traversed by Route 66.

A Route 66 icon is the Wigwam Motel. It was built in 1950 as Wigwam Village Motel Number 6 and is one of two remaining Wigwam motels on Route 66. It consists of nineteen cone-shaped wigwam units complete with modern amenities, outdoor swimming pool, lobby, and giftshop.

WINSLOW

Route 66 originally followed 2nd Street in Winslow. With the post–World War II boom in travel, Route 66 was rerouted into two one-way corridors using 2nd and 3rd Streets.

Preserved at Homolovi State Park, six miles (9.7 km) north of Winslow, are numerous archeological sites framed by quintessential western landscapes. They are vestiges of a civilization that dates to 620 CE. These include four large pueblos, one-room pit houses, and a massive 1,200 room pueblo.

Located about two miles (3.2 km) from present day Winslow is Sunset Crossing on the Little Colorado River. The crossing marks the junction of several historic trails including a pre-Columbian Native American trade route to the coast of California, the Honeymoon Trail used by Mormon immigrants journeying from Utah to northern Arizona settlements during the 1870s, and the Beale Wagon Road.

Established in April 1876 near Sunset Crossing was Brigham City, first called Ballenger's Camp. It was one of four fortified settlements established along the Little Colorado River by Mormon pioneers. They damned the river and built an irrigation system to sustain farming in the river valley. A flour mill was built, and a post office was established in 1879. In 1881, after a series of droughts and floods, the village was abandoned.

In late 1880, a construction camp for the Atlantic & Pacific Railroad was established at the site of Winslow. The town is named for General Edward F. Winslow, president of the St. Louis–San Francisco Railroad, a company that owned half of the Atlantic & Pacific Railroad.

In 1897, the Atchison, Topeka & Santa Fe Railway purchased the western division of the Atlantic & Pacific Railroad. The company then established repair and maintenance facilities in Winslow.

The town was a uniquely diverse community as the railroad hired Americans as well as European immigrants, Navajos, members of other Native American tribes, and Mexican nationals. In the early twentieth century, the city was referenced as "the metropolis of Northern Arizona" in editorials and feature articles published nationally.

Establishment of the National Old Trails Road during the teens

"NOTHING BEHIND ME, EVERYTHING AHEAD OF ME, AS IS EVER SO ON THE ROAD."

—JACK KEROUAC

fueled the growth of a tourism industry initially launched by the railroad. The *Arizona Good Roads Association Illustrated Road Maps and Tour Book* published by the Arizona Good Roads Association in 1913 contained a detailed section on Winslow and area attractions. It also notes available services including The Palace Hotel, "New Throughout." The hotel offered hot and cold water with private baths and steam heat, unusual amenities in the remote area during the time.

In 1926, the National Old Trails Road through Winslow was incorporated into US 66. Then, in 1929, Winslow's airport was transformed into Winslow-Lindbergh Regional Airport, a stop for Transcontinental Air Transport, one of the first passenger air services in the United States. In 1941, the United States Army Air Corps converted the airport into a refueling and repair facility for military aircraft.

Joseph Kasulaitis worked at the airport from 1929 to 1948. In an interview published in *Arizona Highways* magazine, he recalled meeting numerous celebrities including Charles Lindbergh, Amelia Earhart, John Wayne, Mary Pickford, Clark Gable and Carol Lombard, Jimmy Stewart, and Gary Cooper.

The La Posada Hotel is a showpiece along the Route 66 corridor in Winslow. The Fred Harvey Company retained the services of architect Mary Elizabeth Jane Colter to design the hotel. Built in 1929, the construction cost $1 million. The custom furnishings and landscaped grounds manifested the company's desire to establish a premier resort hotel in northern Arizona, an increasingly popular area for tourists.

The hotel and restaurant opened on May 15, 1930, and the *Western Accommodations Directory* published by AAA in 1954 listed the

property as "very good accommodations" and "An attractive Spanish style hotel. Large guest rooms - $3.50 - $12. Suites with living room $25."

Even with a marked increase in Route 66 travel, resultant of the decline in passenger rail travel after World War I and increasing competition from modern chain motels, the hotel closed in 1957. The furnishings specifically designed for the hotel were sold at auction in 1959. The building was then gutted and converted into offices for the Santa Fe Railway. In 1994, when the railroad consolidated operations, the building was scheduled for demolition.

The National Trust for Historic Preservation listed it as an endangered list property. As a result, Allan Affeldt, an historic property preservationist, commenced a three-year negotiation with the railroad to purchase the property. After acquisition, he established La Posada LLC to facilitate a restoration estimated at $12 million. Today, the La Posada property is described on its website as "Hotel, Gardens, Gallery, and Museum."

On May 29th, 1997, the Standin' on the Corner Foundation was formed to develop a park that would commemorate the Eagles' first single, "Take It Easy." Artisans from throughout the country were solicited for proposals. The foundation then settled on two components: a mural and a statue.

The dedication took place on September 10, 1999. The Standin' on the Corner Park included a *trompe-l'œil* mural by John Pugh on the remaining wall of a building destroyed by fire. The life-sized bronze statue of a man with a guitar by Ron Adamson named "Easy" complimented the mural. The addition of a large Route 66 shield on the pavement in the intersection and a vintage Ford flatbed truck completed the park. It has become a destination for Route 66 travelers. In 2016, another bronze statue was added as a memorial for the late musician Glenn Frey.

Tangible links to Route 66 history are plentiful in Winslow. Counted among these are the Falcon Restaurant that opened on July 9, 1955, and Earl's Route 66 Motor Court. This motel originally was opened as the Marble Motel on June 18, 1953, by Rex and Lillian Marble.

One of the more unusual, and interesting, attractions along Route 66 in Winslow is the 9-11 Remembrance Gardens. Located at the junction of Transcon Lane and Old Route 66, this memorial is constructed of actual beams that came from the World Trade towers in New York City.

HERE WE ARE...

ASH FORK

In Ash Fork, Route 66 followed Lewis Street and Park Avenue as two one-way corridors when the traffic flow increased exponentially after World War I. The original alignment of the highway followed Pine Street.

The confluence of three tributaries of Ash Creek was an established campsite for travelers on a pre-Columbian trade route. Father Garces purportedly camped at this site during his expedition in 1776 as did Kit Carson, Antoine Leroux, and Captain Lorenzo Sitgreaves on his 1851 expedition. Likewise with Lt. Edward Fitzgerald Beale as he surveyed the Beale Wagon Road while testing the viability of camels for military transport.

In 1882, a construction camp and siding were established by the Atlantic & Pacific Railroad at the site of Ash Fork. With completion of the railroad to this point, the town grew as a shipping center for agricultural products, flagstone, and lumber. It was also an important supply center.

Completion of a rail line from Ash Fork to Phoenix in March 1895 is considered by historians as the end of the frontier era in Arizona. Unique vestiges of this early railroad history are located east of town.

The Johnson Canyon Railway Tunnel Trail is a popular hike through a scenic canyon and tangible link to Arizona frontier history. The Ash Fork–Bainbridge Steel Dam was constructed in 1895. It was the first large steel dam in the world and one of only three ever built in the United States.

The prominence of Ash Fork as a railroad junction is illustrated by the construction of a large depot and a Fred Harvey restaurant shortly before the turn of the century.

Facing the Parlor House Saloon and the Postal Telegraph Store, the complex was located on the north side of the tracks. It burned in June 1905. The fire also destroyed an adjoining restaurant and water tower. In March 1907, the Escalante Hotel that included a restaurant, newsstand, curio shop, barbershop, and depot opened. It was named for explorer Silvestre Escalante.

Built at a cost of $115,000, it was considered one of the most opulent and modern hotels and restaurants in northern Arizona. Amenities included long distance telephone service, hot and cold running water with private bath, electric lights, and steam heat. Crystal chandeliers were used in the dining room and lobby.

COPPER STATE COURT, ASH FORK, ARIZONA

X721

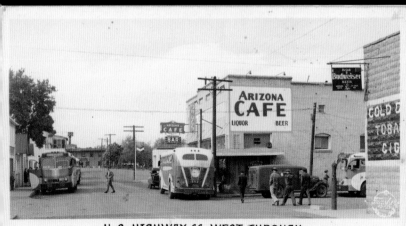

U. S. HIGHWAY 66, WEST THROUGH
ASH FORK, ARIZONA

X724

In his travel journal dated July 15, 1915, Edsel Ford briefly referenced the Escalante and Ash Fork: "Had lunch at Ash Forks Harvey Hotel."

Aside from ranching, tourism, and the railroad, Ash Fork prospered from the quarrying of flagstone. This stone was used extensively during construction of railroad bridges and supports in the late nineteenth and early twentieth century. Many of these can be seen alongside Route 66 in northwestern Arizona.

The town was given the name of "Flagstone Capital of the World" by the Ash Fork Historical Society. The title was officially bestowed upon Ash Fork in 2014 by the Arizona House of Representatives with the passage of H.R. 2001.

Stone was used extensively in the construction of buildings throughout Ash Fork. Examples include the Ash Fork Route 66 Museum that is housed in the historic Arizona Department of Transportation building. Located at 901 W. Old Route 66, it was built in 1922. Another example is the Oasis Lounge at 346 Park Avenue.

As post–World War I traffic on Route 66 increased, passenger rail traffic declined. This and the construction of modern hotels along Route 66 in nearby communities such as Williams resulted in the closure of the Escalante's hotel operations in 1951. Two years later, the restaurant closed. The complex was razed in 1968.

This was the first in a series of blows that decimated the town's economy. Shortly afterward, the Atchison, Topeka & Santa Fe Railway initiated consolidation of maintenance operations and closed facilities in Ash Fork.

In 1977, and again in 1987, two major fires destroyed large sections of the historic business district. Then, in 1979, completion of the I-40 bypass decimated businesses along the Route 66 corridor.

The town has been slow to capitalize on the Route 66 renaissance. Still, there are notable remnants that are tangible links to that highway. There are also new businesses such as Lulu Belle's BBQ at 33 Lewis Avenue that are capitalizing on the town's location as a highway junction and on Route 66.

Copper State Modern Cottages, later renamed Copper State Court, opened for business in 1928. Built by Ezell and Zelma Nelson, it was operated by the same family until 1975.

Main Street
Ash Fork, Arizona

11431

The Hi-Line Modern Auto Court, later renamed Hi-Line Motel, was established in 1936. The complex originally included a Shell station.

Surprisingly, there is also a Hollywood connection with Ash Fork. Released in 1992, *Universal Soldier* starring Jean-Claude Van Damme and Dolph Lundgren had scenes that were filmed in Ash Fork.

This is not the only celebrity association with Ash Fork. In November 1914, the course for the last of the Desert Classic (Cactus Derby) automobile races was charted over the National Old Trails Road from Los Angeles to Ash Fork and then south through Prescott to the finish line in Phoenix. Counted among the entrants in this race were Barney Oldfield, Louis Nikrent, and Louis Chevrolet.

KINGMAN

The pre-1937 alignment of Route 66 followed Front Street, Chadwick Drive, and 4th Street through Kingman. After this date, the highway followed Front Street, which was renamed Andy Devine Avenue during a special episode of *This Is Your Life* in 1955 that profiled character actor Andy Devine.

In January 1880, Lewis Kingman, a survey engineer, was hired by Atlantic & Pacific Railroad to survey a course for the rail line across northern Arizona. In late 1881, railroad contractor Conrad Shenfield working with Kingman established a construction camp at the present site of the city.

A savvy investor, Shenfield negotiated to acquire "town site privileges" from the railroad and began advertising the sale of lots. On January 27, 1883, an advertisement was published in *Alta Arizona*, a weekly territorial newspaper. "For particulars as to prices of town lots in Kingman address C. Shenfield or C.W. Middleton, at Mineral Park (Mohave County seat). A perfect title given soon as the patent for the 160 acres (64.7 ha) upon which the new town is located arrives from Washington."

Initial growth in Kingman was slow. Listed in 1883 tax records was H. W. Coleman who owned a lot with a

tent that he used as a restaurant and W. H. Lake that had two lots on which he had built a house and a saloon. Other commercial properties included a saloon owned by Ryan & Company and a hotel built on two lots.

As Cerbat, Mineral Park, and Stockton Hill, mining camps in the Cerbat Mountains, and the Colorado River port of Hardyville, began to wane, Kingman evolved as the primary transportation, shipping, and commercial center of Mohave County. In 1887, Kingman was designated the county seat.

A frame building was built on Spring Street to house the courthouse. In 1915, with completion of a new courthouse, this building was located to Front Street. It was repurposed as the Commercial Hotel. The hotel would provide lodging for railroad passengers as well as travelers on the National Old Trails Road and Route 66.

On June 10, 1907, construction of a new electrical generation station designed by the Tracy Engineering Company of Los Angeles commenced. The *Mohave County Miner* documented the historic event on July 31, 1909, when the station went online. "The Desert Power and Water Company this week turned

on the juice into their long-distance transmission lines for the purpose of trying them out and 'baking' the transformers."

The plant continued supplying electricity to Kingman and surrounding mining towns until 1938 when the generators at Boulder Dam (Hoover Dam) went online. The renovated facility, now known as the Powerhouse Visitor Center, is home to the Kingman Visitor Center & Gift Shop, the Historic Route 66 Association of Arizona Gift Shop, Bob "Boze" Bell's "The 66 Kid" Exhibition, and an Arizona Route 66 museum. It also houses the Route 66 Electric Vehicle Museum, a collection of electric vehicles on loan from the Historic Electric Vehicle Foundation.

Traffic on the National Old Trails Road, and then Route 66, fueled growth of a service industry that included service stations, garages, motels, and restaurants. It also led to numerous celebrity associations.

On July 16, 1915, Edsel Ford was a guest at the Brunswick Hotel. In 1918, Harry Carey and a film crew used the Hotel Beale as their headquarters while filming *Ace of the Saddle*. This hotel was owned by Thomas Devine, father of character actor Andy Devine. Both hotels were

Hill Top MOTEL

BEST VIEW IN ...NG

Sorry

...TO MART

Amy Kleefeld

THE DEALER WITH A HEART

APPROVED
AAA
MOTEL

REFRIGERATOR ...CRO...
REMOTE TV...H...
FAX   INT...NE...
...UNDROM...T...

ROOMS WITH
ZENITH
CHROMACOLOR TV

El Trovato
MOTEL

ARIZONA

HAVASU FALLS

listed in the *Hotel, Garage, Service Station and AAA Club Directory* published in 1927.

Buster Keaton was a guest at the hotel in 1926 during the filming of *Go West*. In March 1939, Clark Gable and Carole Lombard married at the Methodist Episcopal Church. Movies filmed all or in part in Kingman include *Edge of Eternity*, *Foxfire*, *Roadhouse 66*, *Fear and Loathing in Las Vegas*, and *Two-Lane Blacktop*. While on a photo shoot in Kingman for a 1992 issue of *Playboy Magazine*, Pamela Anderson was read her rights and taken to the police station on charges of indecent exposure.

George Farley "Boots" Grantham played in the 1927 World Series.

During his career spanning the years 1922 to 1934 he played for the Pittsburgh Pirates, as well as the Chicago Cubs, Cincinnati Reds, and New York Giants. He had a long association with the city of Kingman, and on April 1, 1924, he arranged for a game to be played between the Cubs and the Pirates at the county fairgrounds, now the site of Locomotive Park. He is buried in Mountain View Cemetery.

Charles Lindbergh was a frequent guest at the Hotel Beale during construction of Port Kingman, a terminal for Transcontinental Air Transport. He and Amelia Earhart attended the ribbon cutting ceremony for the opening of the terminal on July 8, 1929.

The Kingman airport was established in 1942 as the Kingman Army Airfield, a flexible gunnery school. It operated until 1945 and then was utilized as a storage depot where heavy bombers were scrapped.

Tangible links to Route 66 history are plentiful. They include the Siesta Motel opened in 1929, the Arcadia Lodge, then called the Arcadia Court, opened in 1938, and the Hill Top Motel opened in 1955. The White Rock Court, opened in 1936, was the only motel in Kingman that was listed in the *Green Book* published for Black motorists.

One of the most famous Route 66 locations is Mr. D'z Route 66 Diner, known for their homemade root beer, milkshakes, burgers, and pizza. This restaurant originally opened as the Kimo (KI for Kingman, MO for Mohave County) in 1939.

Aside from Route 66 tourism, Kingman is centrally located to an expansive network of scenic hiking and mountain biking trails. The Monolith Gardens section of the Cerbat Foothills Recreation Area has been deemed a "miniature Monument Valley." Historic Beale Springs, a desert oasis, is also a part of the recreation area as are the historic White Cliffs Wagon Road and the territorial era Taggart Toll Road.

GOLDEN STATE

NEEDLES

Route 66 initially followed the course of the National Old Trails Road along Front Street in Needles. To accommodate the increasing flow of traffic, the highway was later rerouted onto Broadway Street.

There is archeological evidence indicating that the Pipa Aha Macav Mojave tribe, "The People by the River," settled along the Colorado River around present-day Needles several thousand years ago. The Topock Maze (Mystic Maze) near Needles is a geoglyph that is estimated to be more than six hundred years old. It consists of intricate patterns and paths carved into the surface of the desert.

The Mojave people were prolific traders that made use of a trade route west across the Mojave Desert to the Pacific coast and east to villages in present day Arizona and New Mexico. This trade route would become a primary corridor for early American and European explorers. Portions of it would later be incorporated into the Mojave Road, the Beale Wagon Road, the railroad, the National Old Trails Road, and Route 66 as well as I-40 and I-15.

The first European exploration in the area dates to 1604 and the expedition led by New Mexico governor Don Juan de Oñate. In 1775 and 1776, Father Francisco Garces followed the Native American trade route on expeditions in northern Arizona and the Colorado River Valley. He was the namesake for the El Garces Hotel in Needles.

From its inception, Needles was a railroad town. The Atlantic & Pacific Railroad established a station, under the Needles name, and a construction camp on the Arizona side of the Colorado River. With construction of a division point on the California side of the river, a town began to develop. It was also named Needles. In late 1883, the post office application for the Arizona community was amended to indicate a name change to Topock.

The town is named for the sharp mountain peaks, "the Needles," in the Mohave Mountains that run along the Colorado River to the south of town. They were named by Lt. Amiel Weeks Whipple during his topographical survey expedition in 1854.

After the Atchison, Topeka & Santa Fe depot and Fred Harvey Company–managed hotel burned in 1906, the El Garces was built. It opened in 1908 as a passenger and

freight depot with modern hotel and restaurant. Travelers on the National Old Trails Road, and then Route 66, that passed in front of the complex ensured profitability.

Created in the spring of 1942 was the Desert Training Center, an expansive Mohave Desert facility to prepare troops for the invasion of North Africa. Needles served as a supply center, and General Patton used the El Garces as a communication center. It served a similar purpose during Desert Strike military maneuvers in the surrounding desert during the early 1960s.

Resultant of the postwar decline in passenger rail travel and realignment of Route 66, the El Garces closed in 1949. The Atchison, Topeka & Santa Fe Railway demolished a large portion of the complex shortly afterward. The remainder was gutted and converted into railroad offices. In 1988, consolidated railroad operations resulted in closure of the building. By 1993, resultant of abandonment and vandalism, the City of Needles condemned the property as a first step toward razing the building.

In 1993, a local group, Friends of El Garces, formed to preserve and renovate the former hotel. In 2002,

the National Park Service recognized the building's significance by listing it in the National Register of Historic Places. The façade, fountains, and grounds have been renovated as have the interior that is used as an event center.

As the town was a literal desert oasis for travelers on the National Old Trails Road and Route 66, a thriving service industry developed. Jack Rittenhouse, in *A Guide Book to Highway 66*, noted three hotels in addition to the El Garces, seven motels, and numerous garages as well as cafés.

He also noted that during the months of summer, it was advisable to cross the Mojave Desert at night. To accommodate these travelers, many motels offered special day rates. In Edsel Ford's travel journal dated July 17, 1915, he noted, "Started west from Needles at 6:15 P.M. Roads in desert were fair. Stopped for midnight lunch."

Relocation of railroad operations, the bypass of Route 66 with completion of I-40, and construction of the highway 95 Colorado River bridge that connected with Fort Mohave, Arizona, decimated the city's economy. Still, there are landmarks of note.

Valenzuela's is a family-owned restaurant that opened in 1952. Fender's River Road Resort is a motel and RV park complex that opened in about 1960. It is the only motel located on the Colorado River, the National Old Trails Road, and Route 66.

Celebrity association with Needles is long and diverse. Carty's Camp, a complex with gas station, garage, and cabins that was established in 1925, can be seen in the film adaptation of *The Grapes of Wrath*. Charles Schulz, the cartoonist that created the *Peanuts* comic strip, lived in Needles from 1928 through 1929.

A second season episode of the television program *Mission Impossible* entitled "The Town" was filmed in Needles. The movies *Two Lane Blacktop*, 1971, and *Convoy*, 1978, have scenes that were filmed in Needles. First Lady Eleanor Roosevelt spoke at a Needles School District forum.

Needles is the gateway to a diverse array of outdoor recreational opportunities. This includes the Colorado River and the historic Mojave Road which traverses the scenic Mojave National Preserve.

DAGGETT

The earliest alignment of Route 66 in Daggett followed the course of the National Old Trails Road south of the railroad tracks and the primary business district. The latter alignment followed Santa Fe Street and the Daggett Yermo Road.

The namesake for the community is John Daggett, lieutenant governor of California from 1883 to 1887, who platted the town site. He was also the owner of the Bismarck Mine in the Calico Mountains.

The Old Spanish Trail established in 1829 as a trade route between Santa Fe and the pueblo of Los Angeles followed the Mojave River across the western Mojave Desert. The river as an oasis was the catalyst for initial settlement in the immediate area of Daggett in the late 1860s when a scattering of prospector's cabins was built. Originally called Calico Junction, the camp became an important supply center when extensive silver deposits were developed six miles (9.6 km) to the north in the Calico Mountains during the 1870s.

In 1881, the town of Calico was established and quickly boomed with the discovery of the largest silver strike in California to date in the Calico Mountains. Among the largest of the more than 500 mines operating in the area was the Silver King Mine that produced more than $20 million over the next 12 years. The town had a population of more than 1,200 people that were dependent on the supply center at Daggett.

To capitalize on the boom, the Southern Pacific Railroad extended its rail line east from Mojave to Calico Junction (Daggett). Another line was constructed from Needles on the Colorado River. In late 1884, Southern Pacific Railroad leased this line to the Atlantic & Pacific Railroad, a subsidiary of the Atchison, Topeka & Santa Fe Railway. Indicative of Daggett's prominence, the railroad then built a two-story depot with freight yard and warehouses.

Two years prior, the Stone Hotel was built on Santa Fe Street by Victor Van Briesen and George McKenzie. Naturalist John Muir, whose daughter resided in Daggett, was a frequent guest. Walter "Death Valley Scotty" Scott held a permanent reservation for room number 7. The long-closed hotel has survived three fires. After the devastating fire of 1908, the second story was razed.

"The Daggett Garage began life in the 1880s at the borax town of Marion, located on the northeast shore of Calico Dry Lake, as a locomotive repair roundhouse for the narrow-gauge Borate and Daggett Railroad. Daggett blacksmith Seymour Alf used a twenty-mule team to move the building to the Waterloo Mill and mine, southwest of Calico, circa 1896, where it served a similar purpose for a silver ore narrow-gauge railroad. Walter Alf, Seymour Alf's son, moved the building to its current location in Daggett circa 1912."

"The building was an auto repair shop on the National Old Trails Highway until World War II, when it became a mess hall for United States Army troops guarding the local railroad bridges. The Fouts brothers bought the building in 1946 and operated an automotive garage and machine shop in the building until the mid-1980s. The building is currently owned and operated by the Golden Mining and Trucking Company."

As early as 1882, rich deposits of colemanite (calcium borate or borax) had been discovered in Death Valley. Freighting contractors established a network of trails connecting mines, mining camps, and the railroad siding at Daggett. The image of the 20 mule team wagons hauling borax was featured by the Pacific Coast Borax Company in their advertising and in their manufactured line of laundry detergents and cleaners named "20 Mule Team Borax."

The company sponsored *Death Valley Days*, a radio and television anthology series dramatizing stories of the frontier era in the west launched in 1930. From 1952 to 1975, *Death Valley Days* was produced as a syndicated television series. One of Ronald Reagan's last television roles was as the host of the program between 1964 and 1965.

Aside from the Stone Hotel, the Daggett Garage is one of the most significant buildings in town. An historic marker at the garage details its unique history (see left).

Seymour Alf also built a blacksmith shop on 1st Street. It was here that the now famous heavy freight borax wagons were built.

Also of interest is the Desert Market that opened in 1908 and the oddly styled house, known as the Ski Lodge Roof House, at the corner of National Old Trails Road and Daggett-Yermo Road. Verifiable details are scarce but local sources note that this building opened about 1926 as a visitor's information center and was later used as a café. Then, in the late 1930s, it became the home of Mojave Deserts "Poet Laureate" Alice Richards Salisbury. It was announced in 2020 that there were plans for the conversion of the building back into a visitor's center.

Additional information was provided in a feature published by *The Desert Way*. "The old California Agricultural Inspection Station mentioned in John Steinbeck's *The Grapes of Wrath* was located in Daggett right across the road from the ski lodge building, formerly the Minneola Land Development Company sales office."

In Jack Rittenhouse's *A Guide Book to Highway 66*, he noted that Daggett was, ". . . a tree shaded little old town that was formerly the location of smelters which handled the ore brought down from nearby mountains. Some of the old store buildings remain, but the town is now quiet. There are two trailer camps but no cabins. Cafés, garage, and gas stations."

BARSTOW

In Barstow, Route 66 was literally Main Street. Interestingly, at the time of US 66 certification in 1926, this corridor was only a year old. The business district was originally established on the north side of the tracks in the 1880s. In 1925, the Atchison, Topeka & Santa Fe Railway dramatically expanded the rail yard forcing almost the entire town to be moved to the south side of the tracks.

The one exception was the Casa del Desierto. The first hotel and railroad depot on this site was built in May 1887. Two months later in July it was destroyed by fire. A new complex was built but it burned down in 1892. A new hotel and deport was again rebuilt, but it too burned down in 1908.

Designed by talented architect Mary Elizabeth Jane Colter and constructed from 1909 to 1911, the Casa del Desierto was a showpiece for the Fred Harvey Company, the railroad, and for the city of Barstow. The hotel remained in business until 1959 and the restaurant until 1970, which made this one of the last Fred Harvey Company railroad hotels to close.

In 1974, the Atchison, Topeka & Santa Fe Railway initiated plans to raze the complex. A group of concerned Barstow citizens facilitated inclusion of the building on the National Register of Historic Places in 1975. This was the first step in a lengthy series of discussions that resulted in the railroad donating the buildings to the City of Barstow.

A gala celebration was planned to showcase the renovated buildings, deemed the Historic Barstow Harvey House, in 1992. Shortly before the celebrations, the building was damaged in the Landers earthquake. This resulted in a two-year delay and additional repairs.

Housed in the building today is the Route 66 "Mother Road" Museum that was dedicated on July 4, 2000, and the Western America Railroad Museum. It also serves as an Amtrak stop, an office building, and has a ballroom used for social events.

The Barstow area has been the focal point of a transportation network for centuries. A Native American trade route from the Colorado River to the coast of California followed the Mojave River. A portion of this path was incorporated into the Old Spanish Trail that connected Santa Fe in New Mexico with the presidio at Los Angeles.

BARSTOW, CALIF.

Mapping of this trail commenced in 1776 and was officially designated in 1829. John C. Fremont published a report in 1844 about the trail after completing a U.S. Army Corps of Topographical Engineers expedition. After the War with Mexico ended in 1848, the trail fell into disuse as other trails were being developed across northern Arizona. The Old Spanish Trail was officially designated a National Historic Trail when President George W. Bush signed S.1946 on December 4, 2002.

In the late 1840s, the Mormon Road was built connecting Salt Lake City with Los Angeles. It followed sections of the Old Spanish Trail along the Mojave River.

In 1857, an expedition led by Lt. Edward Fitzgerald Beale tasked with establishing a trade route along the 35th parallel from Fort Smith, Arkansas, to Los Angeles, California, followed the Mojave Trail across the Mojave Desert and then to the junction of the Old Spanish Trail and Mormon Road. A small trade center named Fish Ponds on the Mojave River was established around 1860.

In 1882, the Southern Pacific Railroad extended its line from Mojave, established a switchyard, and the village was renamed Lt.

Edward Fitzgerald Beale. The namesake was Robert W. Waterman, governor of California from 1887 to 1891.

The switchyard and junction figured prominently in a battle for control of the southern California rail system and its development. The Atlantic & Pacific Railroad, a subsidiary of the Atchison, Topeka & Santa Fe Railway, built a line across the Mojave Desert. In 1884, the Atchison, Topeka & Santa Fe Railway acquired controlling interest in the California Southern Railroad and plans were made to extend that line from San Bernardino to Waterman Junction.

In 1886, Waterman Junction was renamed Barstow. This was in deference to William Barstow Strong, then the president of the Atchison, Topeka & Santa Fe Railway.

By the 1890s, the waning mining boom in the surrounding mountains and desert left Barstow dependent on the railroad. Though the community prospered as a major railroad maintenance center, in the post-1910 years, an ever-increasing flow of travelers on the National Old Trails Road and Arrowhead Trail that connected Los Angeles with Salt Lake City fueled development of an extensive service industry. Traffic on Route 66 after 1926 further increased reliance on travelers.

In early 1942, the War Department established the Marine Corps Logistics Base (MCLB) at Barstow. During the same period, the U.S. Army assigned General George S. Patton Jr. to prepare troops for the invasion of North Africa. After surveying the southwestern United States for a suitable training site, General Patton and his staff established the boundary of the Desert Training Center.

At 18,000 square miles (46,620 km²) stretching from Barstow through the deserts of southern California, western Arizona, and southern Nevada, this was the largest military training facility in the world. Route 66 communities including Needles, Goffs, Ludlow, Amboy, Essex, Daggett, and Barstow were impacted by creation of the military reservation.

Though Route 66 was bypassed and the businesses along that highway suffered, Barstow remains a major transportation hub. And the Marine Corps base, the only military facility bisected by Route 66, remains an important component in the city's economy.

LOS ANGELES

The original western terminus of Route 66 was the intersection of Broadway and 7th Street in the heart of the city's historic theater district. Over the course of its history, the highway was realigned numerous times. In addition to Broadway, the course of the highway included Arroyo Seco Parkway, Huntington, San Fernando, and Mission.

Among the many things that make Los Angeles County unique is the fact that it is the traditional homeland to three Native American tribes: the Ventureño, Gabrieleño, and Fernandeño. None are recognized by the federal government, but they are recognized by the State of California. It is also home to more Native Americans and Alaska Natives than any other county in the United States.

Spanish explorer Juan Rodriquez Cabrillo is generally credited as being the first European to sail along the coast in this part of California. There is no evidence that his expedition of 1542 came ashore.

El Pueblo de la Reina de Los Angeles (The Town of the Queen of Angels) was officially founded on September 4, 1781. It was a component in Spain's colonization initiative to counter Russian incursions into Alaska, the Pacific Northwest, and northern California that commenced in the 1760s.

The first pioneers to settle in Los Angeles were forty four people from Mexico. As a point of interest, historian Antonio Rios-Bustamante claims that there were "people of Spanish, Mexican, American Indian, and African descent."

El Pueblo de Los Angeles Historical Monument is located near the site of the early Los Angeles pueblo. This is a living museum that attracts more than 2 million visitors annually. It is located a few blocks from Route 66.

Olvera Street immediately to the east is described by Discover Los Angeles as a "colorful traditional Mexican marketplace that opened on Easter Sunday, April 20, 1930, following a preservation campaign." Maintained here are some of the city's oldest buildings that house a variety of homes, store fronts, restaurants, and other businesses.

Originally, Route 66 also traversed the area known as China Town. The first "Chinatown" district was

LOS
GE
THE GRAMMY MUSEUM® PRESENTS
AND THE BIRTH OF PUNK
THE GRAMMY MUSEUM® PRESENTS
AND THE BIRTH OF PUNK

located a few blocks away where Union Station stands today. In the early 1930s, the district was razed for construction of the train terminal. In June 1938, "New Chinatown" celebrated its grand opening. As a point of interest, this is a cultural landmark as it was the first neighborhood in the United States owned by Chinese residents.

The first Chinese immigrants in Los Angeles were documented in 1852. A distinctive Chinese enclave was established by 1857. By 1870, "Chinatown," a district of more than 200 people, had developed between El Pueblo Plaza and Old Arcadia Street. By the late nineteenth century, this area was the center of the city's laundry and produce industries. With exotic restaurants, curio shops, and "strange" entertainments, the district was quite popular with pioneering tourists that arrived in the city by automobile.

When Americans began dominating the city, boosters and land speculators began to sell the first iteration of the "California Dream." A magazine called *Land of Sunshine* was established to promote California's temperate climate, farming opportunities, and exotic culture. Marketing initiatives claimed that this was a place where a new immigrant could

"cheer himself with her almost everlasting sunlight."

Other successful marketing campaigns focused on people with illnesses and maladies. One promotional brochure featured a bold headline that read, "The overworked and over worried class will find here a most soothing climate to regain their lost energy or restore the nervous system to its normal equilibrium."

By the 1880s, a steady stream of immigrants was arriving in the area from the east coast and the Midwest. One of these settlers was Daeida Wilcox, cofounder of Hollywood in 1887.

Commencing in the early twentieth century, the corridor along Broadway that would become Route 66 after 1926 began to develop as the theater district. At its height, this was the densest concentration of theaters in the world.

The six blocks from 3rd to 9th Streets along South Broadway has been designated the Historic Broadway Theatre District. It includes twelve movie theaters built between 1910 and 1931 and was added to the National Register of Historic Places in May 1979. This was the first and largest historic theatre district listed on the register.

LA-45—Daily Crowds — Seventh at Broadway, Los Angeles, California

QB-H2585

The district is also the large concentration of movie palaces remaining in the United States. The Los Angeles Conservancy, the Bringing Back Broadway initiative, the Broadway Theatre Group, and the Los Angeles Historic Theatre Foundation have worked to restore several of the theaters.

Opened February 1, 1918, the "Million Dollar Theatre" was built by Sid Grauman, better known for Grauman's Egyptian Theatre and Grauman's Chinese Theatre. This is located directly across from the landmark Bradbury Building. It is part of the Grand Central Square project that includes the revitalized Grand Central Market.

The Grand Central Market opened in 1917 and except for the COVID-19 pandemic in 2020 has been in continuous operation. The open-air arcade continues to reflect the changing demographic of the district. In the 1920s, more than ninety vendors included green grocers, fishmongers, Jewish delis, butchers, bakers, flower stands, and coffee shops. Today, in addition to the array of shops reflecting the city's rich cultural diversity, the market is a treasure trove of neon signage that spans nearly a century.

IMAGE CREDITS

a = all, b = bottom, i = inset, L = left, r = right, t = top

AUTHOR: p21; p26–27; p38–39; p50–51; p51i; p55; p61; p64–65; p70; p76–77; p79; p84–85; p94–95; p96; p99; p100–101; p103; p104–105; p114–115; p120; p130; p134; p138; p141; p143; p144; p147; p151L; p155; p162; p164–165; p167; p173; p176; p181; p182–183; p187; p189; p197; p198.

GRAYSHADE PHOTOGRAPHY: p24.

JOE SONDERMAN, MIKE WARD & STEVE RIDER COLLECTIONS: p29t&b; p31; p34a; p36; p41; p42; p48; p58; p59; p60; p62; p73; p74; p82; p88; p89; p90; p92; p106; p107; p111; p121; p125; p137; p168t&b; p170; p171; p185; p191t&b; p194; p200.

LORI MALCOLM: p53; p54.

SHUTTERSTOCK: p4, rawf8; p5, Ingo70; p6, Cesar Dussac; p9, Sarnia; p10–11, StockPhotoAstur; p14–15, Eddie J. Rodriquez; p17, Eddie J. Rodriquez; p18–19, Gimas; p22–23, Gimas; p32–33, Randall Runtsch; p35, Eddie J. Rodriquez; p44–45, TLF Images; p47, Gimas; p56–57, Nick Fox; p63, Brian Scantlebury; p66, Gimas; p68–69, Chris Higgins Photography; p71, PhotoTrippingAmerica; p80–81, BD Images; p87, BD Images; p93, 4kclips; p98, Steve Lagreca; p108–109, Andrey Bayda; p110, Steve Lagreca; p112, Logan Bush; p113, Steve Lagreca; p117, Joseph Sohm; p118–119, T photography; p122–123, Andrey Bayda; p127, Svetlana Foote; p128–129, mcrvlife; p131, Fotoluminate LLC; p132–133, Nagel Photography; p135, William Cushman; p136, LizCoughlan; p146, Logan Bush; 148–149, Neil Lockhart; p150, Pixel Doc; p151r, Joseph Sohm; p152–153, DCA88; p156–157, Chris Curtis; p159, Chris Curtis; p161, John Manjeot; p174–175, Michael Gordon; p177, Steve Lagreca; p178–179, Gimas; p192–193, Unai Huizi Photography; p195, Felipe Sanchez.

INDEX

ABOUT THE AUTHOR

Jim Hinckley is the author of more than twenty books on an array of subjects ranging from the history of the American auto industry to Route 66, ghost towns, and travel guides. He has also written feature articles for international and domestic publications including *MotoringNZ*, *Route Trip USA*, *True West*, *Old Cars Weekly*, *Cars & Parts*, and *Route 66*.

Jim and his wife Judy are the creators of Jim Hinckley's America, a multi-faceted platform that includes books, presentations, tourism development projects based community-education programs, a social media network, and tour development. Presentations on Route 66, the American auto industry, and Southwest travel have been made at the first and second European Route 66 festivals, Miles of Possibility Conference, and at museums and events in the United States, Germany, the Netherlands, and the Czech Republic.

Jim and Judy reside in Kingman, Arizona. Jim has served on the city's Historic Preservation Committee and Economic Development Advisory Committee. He also serves on the Route 66 Road Ahead Partnership Economic Development Committee and has provided services as a tourism development consultant for the cities of Cuba, Missouri, and Tucumcari, New Mexico.